A Light to the Gentiles

Books by William C. Mills

Pastoral Ministry

Church, World, and Kingdom: The Eucharistic Foundations of Alexander Schmemann's Pastoral Theology

Kyprian Kern: Orthodox Pastoral Service

Called to Serve: Readings on Ministry From the Orthodox Church

Church and World: Essays in Honor of Michael Plekon

Biblical Prayer and Spirituality

A 30 Day Retreat: A Personal Guide to Spiritual Renewa

Walking with God: Stories of Life and Faith

Come Follow Me

The Prayer of St. Ephrem: A Biblical Commentary

Our Father: A Prayer for Christian Living

Encountering Jesus in the Gospels

Lectionary Series

A Light to the Gentiles: Re ections on the Gospel of Luke

Baptize All Nations: Reflections on the Gospel of Matthew for the Pentecostal Season

Feasts of Faith: Reflections on the Major Feast Days

From Pascha to Pentecost: Reflections on the Gospel of John

Let Us Atend: Reflections on the Gospel of Mark for the Lenten Season

Prepare O Bethlehem: Reflections on the Scripture Readings for the Christmas-Epiphany Season

A LIGHT TO THE GENTILES

*Reflections on
the Gospel of Luke*

William C. Mills

First Published by Orthodox Research Institute, 2008
Reprinted by OCABS Press, 2018

ISBN 1-60191-044-4 (Paperback)

For
Father Sergius and Dina
Thomas, Timothy, Mary

With Friendship, Love, and Affection

PRAYER BEFORE THE GOSPEL

(*From the Divine Liturgy of Saint John Chrysostom*)

Illumine our hearts O Master who loves mankind, with the pure light of Thy divine knowledge. Open the eyes of our mind to the understanding of Thy gospel teachings. Implant also in us the fear of Thy blessed commandments, that, trampling down all carnal desires, we may enter upon a spiritual manner of living, both thinking and doing such things as are well pleasing unto Thee. For Thou art the illumination of our souls and bodies, O Christ our God, and unto Thee we ascribe glory, together with Thy Father, who is from everlasting, and Thine all-holy, good, and life-creating Spirit, now and ever and unto ages of ages. Amen.

TABLE OF CONTENTS

INTRODUCTION

The Orthodox Christian lectionary includes Scripture readings from all four Gospels: Matthew, Mark, Luke, and John, who are also called the four Evangelists. The word evangelist comes from the word "evangelion," meaning good news and from where our English word Gospel comes from. Thus, the four Gospels present to us the good news of salvation which is seen in the preaching, teaching, and ministry of Jesus Christ. The Gospels are not historical accounts or biographies of Jesus, as we have biographies of Abraham Lincoln or Winston Churchill, but present us with the good news of life in Christ. Thus, the Gospels are about faith not history or biography and should be read as such.

A word must be said about Jesus' name. The name Jesus Christ is not a name like John Smith or Jane Doe, Jane being the given name and Doe being the surname. Jesus comes from the Hebrew word Joshua, which comes from the Hebrew name Yeshua, which means savior, and Christ from the Greek word Christos, which means the anointed one. A related word to Christos is the Hebrew term messiah, which also means the anointed one. Thus, when we say Jesus Christ, we actually are saying, "Jesus the anointed one." This information is very important because it clearly defines who we are talking about, Jesus is the anointed one of God who has come to bring God's salvation to the world.

Moreover, Christians believe that God actually took on human form or flesh, or as John the Evangelist puts it, "The Word became flesh and dwelt among us full of grace and truth; we have beheld His glory, glory as of the only Son from the Father" (John 1:14). Our faith is in a particular human person Jesus who was both human and divine and was given all power and authority from God. Everything that we need to know regarding Jesus, His teaching, preaching, and miracles, are contained in the documents called the four Gospels.

The Gospels tell us many things about Jesus. That He was born in the village of Bethlehem sometime early in the first century of the common era from the Virgin Mary who received the good news from the Angel Gabriel, "Do not be afraid Mary, for you have found favor with God. And behold you will conceive in your womb and bear a son, and you shall call His name Jesus" (Luke 1:31). Mary was awe-struck by this good news and she responded with a yes to God which was a yes to all humanity. Mary gave birth to the Son of God who came to save us from our sins.

We also know that Jesus grew up in the village of Nazareth, which is located in northern Israel (Palestine) and He most likely followed in the footsteps of His adopted human father Joseph who is commonly thought to have been a carpenter. However, many scholars now think that Joseph was most likely a stonemason due to the fact that Nazareth was a small village adjacent to the new Roman city called Sepphoris. Today, archeologists and scholars are investigating the remains of this once great Roman city and are rethinking the technology and workmanship in early antiquity. Thus, perhaps Joseph and Jesus may have helped build this new city since it was erected during the time when Jesus, Mary, and Joseph would have lived in Nazareth.

After Jesus was baptized in the Jordan River by John the Baptist, He called the twelve disciples who followed Him throughout the Galilee area, witnessing to His preaching, teaching, and miracles. Later Jesus also sent them out to continue His ministry to the whole world, proclaiming the good news to the far ends of the earth. We know that Jesus was eventually betrayed, arrested, and crucified by the Roman governor Pontius Pilate, suffered, was buried, and was raised from the dead and sits at the right hand of God the Father. At the time of Pentecost, the Holy Spirit was sent into the world to inspire and encourage people to live out their faith in Jesus until the Lord comes again to judge the whole world. Until that time we are called to live our faith in our life, walking the narrow way to the kingdom one step at a time. We encounter the good news of Jesus Christ in the Gospels which we hear every Sunday and which we hopefully read on our own time for prayer and inspiration.

L UKE AND THE FOUR GOSPELS. Matthew, Mark, and Luke are called the Synoptic Gospels. The word synoptic means seen together or seen with. While we have four different Gospels, three of them, Matthew, Mark, and Luke share some common material among them, primarily, the baptism of Jesus, the miracle of the walking on the water, the feeding of the five thousand, Jesus' transfiguration before His disciples, and His death and resurrection. John is not considered a synoptic Gospel since the majority of his Gospel has different material included in it, although John, as with the synoptic Gospels also contains common material such as the feeding of the five thousand and the crucifixion and resurrection accounts.

Overall, we should not be surprised or upset that the four Gospels contain slightly different material. The Evangelists wrote their four accounts as good news to the world, they did not set out to write a detailed biographical story about the life and legacy of Jesus. In other words they do not offer us a detailed snapshot of Jesus, giving us precise details of His life, what He ate, where He went to school, or the type of clothes that He wore. We always need to keep in mind that even though we may be interested in where Jesus went and what He wore, the most important thing to remember is that our faith is in Jesus' Gospel to the world, which is summarized in the two great commandments: love of God and love of neighbor.

One of the earliest testimonies to the four Gospels comes from the writings of the second century Christian Bishop Irenaeus of Lyons. Irenaeus devoted much of his life arguing with Christians who taught a distorted version of Jesus and who were later called heretics. In his book, *Against the Heresies,* Irenaeus gives us information regarding the four Gospels: "Matthew also issued a written Gospel among the Hebrews in their own dialect, while Peter and Paul were preaching in Rome, and laying the foundations of the Church. After their departure, Mark, the disciple and interpreter of Peter did also hand down to us in writing what had been preached by Peter. Luke also, the companion of Paul, recorded in a book the Gospel preached by him. Afterwards, John, the disciple of the Lord, who also had leaned upon His breast, did himself publish a Gospel during his residence at Ephesus in Asia."[1] Irenaeus is one of the earliest Christian writers who attests to the tradition of the four Gospels.

Furthermore, the Church looks to these Gospels as the good news for our edification, for reproof and correction, for our spiritual nourishment, and ultimately for our salvation. The Gospels are so important that they are read during many of our liturgical services, especially the Sunday Divine Liturgy. At every Divine Liturgy, we hear from one of the Gospels and on special days, such as the commemoration of an important saint or a feast day, we may hear more than one Gospel lesson. During Holy Week, we hear a lot from the four Gospels, especially on Holy Thursday and Friday, where we hear the passion account from all four Gospels. Very often the Gospel book is taken in procession around the Church and is venerated during the liturgical services. When the consecration of a new bishop takes place, the gospel book is placed on top of the candidates head as a symbol of his teaching ministry but also that the candidate is being set apart as a bishop in order to teach and proclaim the truth of the Gospel to his flock. Since the Gospels are so important, they are always kept on the altar table where it remains until it is moved by the deacon or priest.

Likewise, the Scriptures are such a source of inspiration and encouragement for the Church that many of the great saints in antiquity wrote sermons and commentaries on the Gospels. These writings of the Church Fathers are also inspiring because we gain additional

---

[1] Irenaeus, *Against the Heresies*, 3.1.

insight when reading their sermons and commentaries, especially those by John Chrysostom, Augustine of Hippo, Cyril of Jerusalem, Gregory the Great, Leo of Rome, and Cyril of Alexandria, among others. Their sermons and writings on the Scriptures are now being translated into English, some of which are included in the appendix in the back of this book. The Scriptures were their spiritual food and nourishment which sustained their preaching, teaching, and pastoral care. They were drawn to the Scriptures as a source of their ministry. If the Scriptures were important to them, hopefully they will be as important for us today! Now more then ever, the Orthodox Christian Church needs to have good scriptural preaching, teaching, and catechesis focusing on the biblical God whose son is Jesus Christ. This learning must take place primarily in our seminaries but also in our parishes and missions. The Scriptures should not be relegated as something optional, but the way in which we seek Jesus the Christ, the Son of God who comes to us through his word which is the Word of Life. Thus, this Word of God must be learned by everyone in the Church, so that we all can grow in faith and in spiritual understanding. Hopefully we too, like the Fathers of the Church, take the Scriptures seriously and draw from the deep well of the waters of life that sustains and nourishes us in the dry deserts and valleys in which we find ourselves.

THE GOSPEL OF LUKE IN THE CHURCH YEAR. The Gospel of Luke is read throughout a large portion of the liturgical year, from mid-September until the feast of the Nativity of Our Lord (Christmas). Luke is also read during the three of the four preparatory Sunday's before Great Lent. We also hear from the Gospel of Luke at the feast of the Annunciation of the Theotokos on March 25 and most of the feast days that are dedicated in her honor; her Nativity on September 8, her Dormition or Falling Asleep on August 15, and her entrance into the Temple in Jerusalem on November 21. We also read the Gospel of Luke at the Feast of the Ascension of our Lord Jesus Christ, during some of the services surrounding the feast of the Nativity of our Lord on December 25, at the Feast of the Meeting of the Lord in the Temple on February 2, as well as on the feast of the birth of John the Baptist on June 24. The reader is encouraged to consult a lectionary for the additional readings from Luke and from the other three Gospels.[2]

Furthermore, the Gospel of Luke contains many parables and stories that are familiar to us: the parable of the Good Samaritan, the parable of the Publican and the Pharisee, the parable of the Rich Man and Lazarus, as well as Jesus' encounter with Zachaeus. Similarly, many of the liturgical hymns throughout the year are taken directly from Luke: the Magnificat, also known as the Song of Mary, which is sung during the Matins service, the *Nunc Dimitis* or also known as the Prayer of St. Symeon, which is sung or read at Great Vespers, and the *Gloria in Excelsis*, which is also sung at the Matins service as well as recited by the priest at in the introduction to the Divine Liturgy.[3] The reader is encouraged to pay close attention to the hymns and prayers throughout the liturgical year, as we will hear many direct or indirect references to the Gospel of Luke.

While the name Luke is not directly mentioned in the Gospel that is attributed to him, we know from the writings of the Apostle Paul that he was Paul's travel companion during missionary trips and was a physician, "For I bear him witness that he has worked hard for you and for those in Laodicea and in Hieropolis. Luke the beloved physician and Demas greet you" (Colossians 4:14), and "Luke alone is with me. Get Mark and bring him with you; for his is very useful

---

[2] Throughout the year, major parts of all four Gospels are read in the Church; from the feast of Pascha until Pentecost we read from the Gospel of John, from Pentecost until mid-September we read from the Gospel of Matthew, and between Epiphany and Great Lent we hear from the Gospel of Mark. Mark is also read on the weekends during Great Lent as well as on some feast and saints days.

[3] The Magnificat is adapted from Luke 1:46–55 and begins "My soul magnifies the Lord and my spirit rejoices in God my savior;" the Prayer of St. Symeon is from Luke 2:29–32 and begins, "Lord, now lettest Thou Thy servant depart in peace;" and the *Gloria in Excelcis* is from Luke 2:14, which begins "Glory to God in the highest."

in serving me" (2 Timothy 4:11). Finally, Luke is mentioned in Paul's epistle to Philemon, "Epaphras, my fellow prisoner in Christ Jesus, sends greetings to you, and do Mark, Aristarchus, Demas, and Luke, my fellow workers" (Philemon 24). Luke's memory is commemorated every year on October 18.

Furthermore, Luke is a Greek name which is also known as Lucas which means light. Most biblical scholars agree that the Gospel of Luke was directed towards a predominately Greek speaking Gentile audience especially since the Gospel is addressed to a certain Theophilus whose name means the lover of God whose name also appears at the beginning of the Book of Acts which is also attributed to Luke:

> In as much as many have undertaken to compile a narrative of the things which have been accomplished among us, just as they were delivered to us by those who from the beginning were eyewitnesses and ministers of the word, it seemed good to me also, having followed all things closely for some time past, to write an orderly account for you, most excellent Theophilus, that you may know the truth concerning the things of which you have been informed (Luke 1:1–4).

> In the first book, O Theophilus, I have dealt with all that Jesus began to do and teach, until the day when He was taken up, after He had given commandment through the Holy Spirit to the apostles whom He had chosen. To them He presented Himself alive after His passion by many proofs, appearing to them during the forty days, and speaking of the Kingdom of God (Acts 1:1–3).

Presumably the author of the book of Acts is also referring to his first book which is the Gospel of Luke, since both books are addressed to Theophilus. Also, Luke describes in detail many of the Jewish religious practices and customs which also leads us to believe that he was writing to a predominately Gentile audience who would have been unfamiliar with the details of Jewish rites and rituals during this time.

In the Scriptures, the Gentiles are often referred to as the nations who were non-Jews. In the Old Testament, we hear about Israel who are God's chosen people, but we also hear about the Gentiles or nations who are also under God's authority, but who are not part of Israel; the Egyptians, Assyrians, Babylonians, and Hittites. Sometimes God actually sends some of Israel's neighbors to attack them in order to bring Israel to repentance and contrition of heart. In other words, even the nations are under God's ultimate control and authority!

Furthermore, according to the Scriptures, the good news of salvation and the invitation to accept Jesus Christ as the savior of the world was offered to both Jews and the Gentiles which is highlighted in the prayer of Symeon the Elder as found in the following passage which is also the inspiration of the title of this book:

> Lord, now lettest Thou Thy servant depart in peace, according to Thy word; for mine eyes have seen Thy salvation which Thou hast prepared in the presence of all peoples, a light for revelation to the Gentiles and for the glory of Thy people Israel (Luke 2:29–32).

This passage from Luke actually echoes an earlier passage in the Book of Isaiah, where he speaks about Israel being a light to the nations, "It is too light a thing that you should be my servant to raise up the tribes of Jacob and to restore the preserved of Israel; I will give you as a light to the nations, that my salvation may reach to the end of the earth" (Isaiah 49:6–7). However, Luke tell us that Mary's son Jesus will be the light to the Gentiles as He came preaching and teaching the Kingdom of God, healing the sick and the suffering, and restoring people to physical health. He welcomed the stranger, ate with sinners and prostitutes, and even raised the dead. In the Gospel of John, Jesus tells the crowds that He is the "light of the world" (John 9:5). In Matthew, Jesus teaches that one cannot put a light under a bushel but must put it on top of the table for everyone to see (Matthew 5:15–16). Thus, the Gospel of Luke presents Jesus as the light to the Gentiles, or the nations, which is supposed to be proclaimed and affirmed in every generation. Hopefully we will embrace Luke's message of salvation and not only hear it, but also live and fulfill this message of joy and gladness.

In the appendix to this book, I have included selected sermons from John Chrysostom, Cyril of Alexandria, and Augustine of Hippo in order to introduce the reader into the insights of the Church Fathers on how they read and used the Scriptures. These Church Fathers have left us with an abundance of scriptural commentaries, sermons, theological treatises, as well as pastoral letters as resources for further study and reflection. Many of these writings are now being translated into English and hopefully in the future more material will be available to the public. When reading the selected sermons, it is important not only to read for information or content, but also the form in which the sermon is presented. In other words, we try to see how they made connections between the scriptural text and life. The Fathers spoke about repentance, prayer, baptism, marriage and family life, and the proper understanding of wealth and material possessions. For the Fathers, the Scriptures became the framework or foundation from which they constructed their vision of the Church, drawing from the Scriptures for their preaching, teaching, and ministry. Hopefully we can also return to the Scriptures to once again see how we can follow Christ in our daily life.

A final note is needed about the content of this book. While the Gospel of Luke is read daily from mid-September to the feast of the Nativity of our Lord, as well on other feast days throughout the Church year, *A Light to the Gentiles* only includes the Sunday Gospel readings. However, the reader is encouraged to consult an Orthodox liturgical calendar for the daily readings from Luke. Also, the reader can find further reflections on the Gospel of Luke, especially for the Nativity Season in my previous book, *Prepare O Bethlehem.*

Parishioners and friends have enquired as to why I am devoted to writing books on the Bible. The answer is simple. My experience in parish life has revealed that many people are confused, ignorant, scared, or have very little interest in the Bible and Bible study. Many people have what is called "DBS" or Dusty Bible Syndrome; they own Bibles but never read them! Therefore, in order to help people better understand the Bible, or at least not be scared of opening the book, I set out to provide other Orthodox Christians with short pastoral reflections on books of Scripture so that they will have a better appreciation for the Word of God and begin a life-long study and reading of it.

I also hope that people regularly participate in personal or small group Bible studies, parish retreats, or adult education programs on subjects of the Bible. There are so many ways in which we can study the Scriptures, both privately and communally, all we have to do is put or minds to it and make the Scriptures a part of our prayer and study habits. Furthermore, I hope that *A Light to the Gentiles* will further advance the Word of God in the Orthodox Church so that we will continue preaching, teaching, and studying the Word of God until the Lord returns. I have included additional resources for Scripture study in the bibliography section.

One of the great "lights" in my life is my longtime friend and co-worker in the Lord's Vineyard, Father Sergius Halvorsen and his family, to whom this book is dedicated. His personal commitment to the proclamation of the Word of God is commendable and has been a continual source of courage and inspiration in my own life and ministry. Furthermore, my parishioners at Nativity of the Holy Virgin, especially the members of the St. Innocent Prayer Group, have been a great source of encouragement. Likewise, a word of thanks is due to my family; especially Taisia and my daughters Hannah and Emma. Finally, I am grateful for our diocesan bishop, His Eminence DMITRI, Archbishop of Dallas and the South, for his support and encouragement in my writing endeavors and who always seeks to proclaim the Gospel in both word and deed.

CHAPTER ONE

THE CALLING OF THE DISCIPLES

(LUKE 5:1–11)

Let us praise with sacred songs the holy Apostle Luke,
The recorder of the joyous Gospel of Christ
And the scribe of the Acts of the Apostles;
For his writings are a testimony of the Church of Christ.
He is the physician of human weaknesses and infirmities.
He heals the wounds of our souls,
And constantly intercedes for our salvation!
(*Troparion for the Feast of St. Luke*)

It is appropriate that the first Gospel lesson that we encounter during our readings from the Gospel of Luke is Jesus calling the disciples. This lesson is also found in the Gospels of Matthew 4:18–22, Mark 1:16–20, and John 1:35–51. In the account from Matthew and Mark, Jesus walks by the Sea of Galilee and sees both Peter and his brother Andrew mending their nets. Jesus invites them to follow Him and they drop what they are doing and follow Him. Soon thereafter, James and his brother John of Zebedee also encounter the Lord and they too follow Jesus. According to the Gospel of John, two disciples of John the Baptist were standing nearby and when they saw Jesus He said to them "Come and see." Andrew was one of the disciples who first met Jesus and then he went and got his brother Simon Peter. Later both Nathaniel and Philip came as well. Nathaniel even makes the bold statement about Jesus that is only found in the Gospel of John, "Rabbi, You are the Son of God! You are the King of Israel!" (John 1:49). We are not given any more information about these men other than that they were fishermen. According to the Gospel tradition, the disciples must have known each other at least informally since Jesus found them working together.

In Luke's version of the calling story, we have a somewhat different recollection of events. This Gospel lesson immediately follows a cycle of two miracles, the cleansing of unclean spirits from a man in the synagogue and the healing of Peter's mother-in-law who was ill (Luke 4:31–39). After witnessing these two miracles, many people came searching for Jesus because they encountered His power and authority. People were crowding around Jesus as Peter and Andrew were mending their nets by the lake of Genesseret, which is also known as the Sea of Galilee. The Sea of Galilee is in Northern Palestine from which the River Jordan flows from the north to the south, dividing the land into two parts. To the south is Jerusalem and to the west is the Mediterranean Sea. The Gospel of John also refers to the Sea of Galilee as the Sea of Tiberias who was a very powerful Roman Emperor during the time of Jesus.

Furthermore, it is important to know that the Galilee area was populated primarily by non-Jewish peoples, called Gentiles. Gentiles were considered unclean according to the traditions of Judaism and the Jews did not socialize or interact with them. Yet in the opening chapter of Luke, Jesus says that He was not just sent only to the Jews but also to the Gentiles (Luke 4:18–19). The Gospel was preached to both the Jews as well as to the Gentiles, which goes back to the Old Testament as we see in this passage from the Prophet Isaiah:

> Arise, shine; for your light has come, and the glory of the Lord has risen upon you. For behold, darkness shall cover the earth, and thick darkness the peoples; but the Lord will arise upon you, and his glory will be seen upon you. And nations shall come to your light, and kings to the brightness of your rising. Lift up your eyes round about, and see; they all gather together, they come to you; your sons shall come from far, and your daughters shall be carried in the arms. Then you shall see and be radiant, and your heart shall thrill and rejoice; because the abundance of the sea shall be turned to you, the wealth of nations shall come to you (Isaiah 60:1–5).

Here Isaiah speaks about God's glory filling the whole world, which will be a light to the nations. Isaiah says that the messiah will come and proclaim the good news to the poor, the orphan, and the widow, and will bring peace on earth, a theme which Luke picks up and develops in the birth narratives (Luke 1–3). In the second chapter of Luke, the elder Symeon picks up the Christ child in his arms and proclaims that this child will be a light to the nations. Throughout the first few chapters of Luke, Jesus is seen in Galilee, preaching, teaching, and performing miracles to the Gentiles.

When Jesus encountered Peter and Andrew, He got into a boat and set a little from the shore and taught the people. This was a very practical way to teach large crowds of people. In the ancient world, microphones were not available, so people used natural sources such as the water which transmitted sounds across a great distance. Similarly, archeologists have unearthed large outdoor amphitheaters which were either hewn out of the side of a hill, very much like our modern day stadium seating at sports events and in large movie theaters. The actors stood at the bottom of the amphitheater where there would be a large stage erected. When the actors used a normal speaking voice the sound could be heard across the large amphitheater which could sometimes hold thousands of people. This is very similar to what Jesus did on the lake of Genesseret.

After Jesus taught the crowds, He told the disciples to out into the deep water for a catch of fish. Luke tells us that the disciples had fished all night and did not catch anything. However, as they put out into the deep water they were amazed at the great catch of fish, a story very reminiscent of John 21:4–8, where Peter and the other disciples caught a large catch of fish. In the Lukan account, after Peter witnessed the great catch of fish he declared, "Depart from me, for I am a sinful man, O Lord" (Luke 5:8). The Gospel concludes as Jesus tells them, "Do not be afraid: henceforth you will be catching men." And when they had brought their boats to land, they left everything and followed Him" (Luke 5:11). After Peter encountered the power of the Lord, He realized that he was a sinner. Before Peter met Jesus, he relied on his own strength and power to catch fish, yet, at Jesus' word, Peter and the other disciples brought in a large catch of fish, more than they ever expected!

We can learn some very important lessons from today's Gospel reading. First, that the great catch of fish immediately follows after Jesus taught the people. The Gospels speak about Jesus as a Teacher or as John calls him "Rabbi," which is the Hebrew word for teacher. During the time of Jesus, the leader in the community called the rabbi who was the one who read and studied the Scriptures and who was capable of teaching others. Later, the sayings of these famous rabbi's were written down so that their teachings would be studied by future generations.

Throughout the Gospels, the Pharisees were the ones who tried to trap Jesus in His own teachings. Among the most popular of the Pharisees was the Apostle Paul, formerly known as Saul. In his epistle to the Galatians, he tells us that he was a Pharisee who sat at the feet of the famous Rabbi Gamaliel in Jerusalem and learned and studied the Law, "If any other man thinks he has reason for confidence in the flesh, I have more: circumcised on the eighth day, of the people of Israel, of the tribe of Benjamin, a Hebrew born of Hebrews; as to the law a Pharisee, as to zeal a persecutor of the church, as to righteousness under the law blameless" (Philippians 3:5–6. See also Acts 9:1–2, 1 Cor. 15:9, and Gal. 1:13). We also know of other noteworthy Pharisees such as Nicodemus who visits Jesus by night questioning him about eternal life (John 3:1–15).

The Saducees were also a Jewish group and leaders of the Jews but they differentiated from the Pharisees in that they were of the aristocracy and they did not believe in the general resurrection from the dead and angels, both of which the Pharisees believed. Furthermore, the Scriptures often mention the scribes. The scribes were highly trained and skilled Jews whose job was to copy the scrolls of the Old Testament. The people did not have printing presses or computers during those times so they had to write everything by hand using a stylus which was a sharp piece of wood, very much like our pencils which they used to write on scrolls which were then kept in the synagogues.

Two more groups of Jews are important to discuss, the Essenes and the Zealots. The Essenes were a group of Jews who lived an austere live of fasting, prayer, and community life. They hated the Romans and were earnestly awaiting their demise. They mostly lived near the area of the Dead Sea in Palestine. They wrote down various rules of their life which were hidden in large water jars in the Dead Sea desert and were eventually found by a Bedouin shepherd in the mid 1940's. These scrolls give us some insight into the daily life of these Essenes and are called the Dead Sea Scrolls. The Zealots are also mentioned a few times in the Gospels and they were the political group who wanted to use force to overthrow the Roman government. All of this information helps us to better understand the religious and social world of Jesus and the message of the Gospel.

According to the Gospels, Jesus was a teacher who taught people about forgiveness, love, compassion, and mercy. In the Gospel of Matthew, Jesus sat down on the mountain and delivered what we call the Sermon on the Mount, which is a series of teachings on prayer, almsgiving, fasting, and love. It is here in the Sermon on the Mount where we find the Lord's Prayer, the only prayer that is given to us by Jesus Himself (Matthew 5–7). In the beginning of Luke, we see Jesus teaching in the synagogue and as Luke emphasizes, "as was His custom." Likewise, at the end of the Gospel of Luke, the risen Jesus appears to Cleopas and an unnamed disciple who were on their way to the village of Emmaus after the crucifixion of Jesus. They told Jesus that they did not understand what had taken place. Jesus then answered them, "'O foolish men, and slow to heart to believe all that the prophets have spoken! Was it not necessary that the Christ should suffer these things and enter into His glory?' And beginning with Moses and all the prophets, He interpreted to them all the Scriptures the things concerning Himself" (Luke 24:25–27, 8:21, and 11:28). In other words, the risen Jesus was still their teacher as He instructed them about both the law and the prophets.

Second, the fisherman were sent out into the deep waters where they caught a big shoal of fish, more so than they had previously caught. Prior to meeting Jesus, they were satisfied with catching fish from the shallow waters around the edge of the lake. However, after Jesus sent them into the deep waters, they caught two boat-loads of fish! They were sent out far into the open waters where there were great waves and where storms were very powerful. Yet it is here, in the outer regions of the lake where the disciples found the great catch of fish which is a metaphor for catching men for the Kingdom. The Old Testament refers to God to as a fisherman who catches men for the kingdom, "For Thou makest men like the fish of the sea, like crawling things that have no ruler. He brings all of them up with a hook, he drags them out with his net, he gathers them in his seine" (Habakkuk 1:14–15) and "Behold, I am sending for many fishers, says the Lord, and they shall catch them" (Jeremiah 16:16).

Third, Luke tells us that these disciples had dropped everything and followed Jesus. They left their house and home, their regular routines of life, their friends, and their financial well-being, all in order to follow the Lord. They left their familiar way of life in obedience to Jesus Christ. The Old Testament is full of stories where God calls people and they want to flee in the other direction, especially Moses, Jonah, Jeremiah, and Amos. Hearing God's voice and obeying it is very difficult, but the Lord does have a way of being very convincing!

This short Gospel lesson is truly powerful. Jesus raises the bar for evangelism, not only for the first disciples but also for us. In the past decades we have been quite satisfied with increased membership in our missions and Churches due to Orthodox Christians who have either moved or relocated to our neighborhoods or through the baptism of young children. However, this is easy type of fishing, the fishing that the disciples did before going out into the deep waters. It is one thing to stand by the shore of the lake and to cast the net. However, it is quite another to go out into the vast deep water and cast ones net. Yet it is here where the great catch of fish is waiting.

If the great catch of people is in the deep waters, should not we as Orthodox faithful go beyond our mission and parish neighborhoods and reach out to the communities around us? We have a mandate to

"Go therefore and make disciples of all nations, baptizing them in the name of the Father and of the Son and of the Holy Spirit, teaching them to observe all that I have commanded you; and lo, I am with you to the close of the age" (Matthew 28:19–20). Of course the answer is yes! The Lord has promised us that our job is to go out into the vast wide treacherous oceans that surround our parishes and reach out for a large catch. There are so many people in our world who have not heard Jesus Christ or who have been introduced to a messed up version of Jesus that they do not want to belong to a mission or parish community. However, if we take the time to learn about the Jesus in the Scriptures, and if we go out into the vast dark deep ocean and talk with these people and answer their questions in an open and forthright way we might be surprised at the results. People may actually want to learn more and "come and see" what we are talking about. They might want to "come and see" Jesus as he is proclaimed in the Gospels and worshipped in Church.

Real Church growth will occur when we begin bringing non-Christians into the fold, our modern day Gentiles of which they are many. Yet the major reason we do not go out into the deep waters is due to fear, laziness, or even worse, complacency. Basically many parishes and missions are satisfied with the *status quo* and do not want to go out of their way to bring others into their communities. As Orthodox Christians we are too content with remaining closed in on ourselves, living a self-contained life. We often speak of the parish as being comprised of our people or our group rather than being God's people. If we do not reach out and bring the good news to the world our faith communities will certainly die a slow and painful death. Yet Jesus tells us that the opposite is true: the Gospel will grow and flourish. May we always be obedient servants of Christ and follow Him into the seas and oceans around us seeking to catch people for the Kingdom.

CHAPTER TWO

THE SERMON ON THE PLAIN
(Luke 6:31–36)

Let us praise the godly Luke;
He is the true preacher of piety,
The orator of ineffable mysteries
And the star of the Church,
For the Word who alone knows the hearts of men,
Chose him, with the wise Paul, to be a teacher of the Gentiles!
(*Kontakion for the Feast of St. Luke*)

In the beginning of the Gospel of Matthew, Jesus goes up a high mountain and delivers what we now call the "Sermon on the Mount." This sermon is quite long and goes for three chapters (Matthew 5–7). In this sermon, we hear about the right attitude for prayer, fasting, forgiveness, as well as almsgiving, and the proper way to live together as community. We are presented with a long litany of ethical and moral teachings in the "Beatitudes" which we hear every Sunday in what is often called the Third Antiphon:

Blessed are the poor in spirit, for theirs is the kingdom of heaven
Blessed are those who mourn, for they shall be comforted
Blessed are the meek, for they shall inherit the earth
Blessed are those who hunger and thirst for righteousness,
for they shall be satisfied
Blessed are the merciful, for they shall obtain mercy
Blessed are the pure in heart, for they shall see God.
Blessed are the peacemakers, for they shall be called the sons of God
Blessed are those who are persecuted for righteousness sake, for theirs in the kingdom of heaven

Blessed are you when men revile you and persecute you and
utter all kinds of evil against you falsely on my account.

Rejoice and be glad, for your reward is great in heaven.
(Matthew 5:3–12)

The Sermon on the Mount is also where we find the only prayer
that we have from Jesus Himself which we call the Lord's Prayer. The
sermon presents Jesus as the great teacher who comes and teaches
His disciples about the basic tenants of the Gospel and how we are to
live and share this Gospel with others.

However, in the Gospel of Luke we have this same sermon but in a
different form. Scholars have called it the Sermon on the Plain because
rather than sitting on the mountaintop, Jesus comes down and preach-
es to His disciples on a level place which is a plain or flat area. The
sermon is very similar to the Sermon on the Mount, but Luke divides
it into two parts, a series of blessings followed by a series of woes.

In the Old Testament the woe is a word that is used throughout
the prophetic books to show anger towards those who are not following the will of God. Very often the prophets use the woe against the
rich and the powerful who are not taking care of the poor, widows,
orphans, and those without help, "Woe to those who are ease in Zion,
and to those who feel secure on the mountain of Samaria, the notable
men of the first of the nations, to whom the house of Israel come!"
(Amos 6:1) and "Woe to those who lie upon the beds of ivory, and
stretch themselves upon their couches, and eat lambs from the flock"
(Amos 6:4). The use of the woe is a way to draw attention to the real
tragic nature of life which highlights the differences between the rich
and the poor and so forth:

Blessed are you poor, for yours is the Kingdom of God
Blessed are you that hunger now, for you shall be satisfied
Blessed are you that weep now, for you shall laugh
Blessed are you when men hate you, and when they exclude
you and revile you, and cast you out your name as evil, on
account of the Son of man!

Rejoice in that day, and leap for joy, for behold, your reward is great in heaven, for so their fathers did to the prophets.

But woe to you that are rich, for you have received your consolation.
Woe to you that are full now, for you shall hunger.
Woe to you that laugh now, for you shall mourn and weep
Woe to you, when all men speak well of you, for so their fathers did to the false prophets
(Luke 6:20–26)

The rest of the Sermon on the Plain includes additional teachings such as loving others unconditionally, a teaching which is mentioned in today's Gospel lesson. The entire Scriptures, both the Old and New Testament, can be summed up in the reading for today: love. When we hear the word love we might think of chocolates, greeting cards, or flowers. We also might think of wedding anniversaries, birthdays, and, of course, St. Valentine's Day. Greeting cards and chocolates are wonderful ways to express kindness and love; however, this is not what the Lord is speaking about in the Gospel reading. This type of love is a sacrificial, self-giving love. The Apostle Paul sums it up best when he explains love to the Corinthian community, "Love is patient and kind; love is not jealous or boastful; it is not arrogant or rude. Love does not insist on its own way; it is not irritable or resentful; it does not rejoice at wrong but rejoices in the right. Love bears all things, believes all things, hopes all things, endures all things" (I Corinthians 13:4–7).

Christians are called to love God with all our heart, soul, mind, and strength, and our neighbor as ourselves. This does not mean that we can separate these two commandments and love our neighbor and not God or vice versa; both commandments are intimately connected as we see in the epistle of John, "Beloved, let us love one another; for love is of God, and he who loves is born of God and knows God. He who does not love does not know God; for God is love. In this the love of God was made manifest among us, that God sent His only Son into the world, so that we might live through Him" (1 John 4:7–10) and "If any one says, 'I love God,' and hates his brother, he is a liar: for he who does not love his brother whom he has seen, cannot love God whom he has not seen. And this commandment we have from Him, that he who loves God should love his brother also" (1 John 4:20–21). Thus it is love for God that we come to love and serve our neighbor and it is through loving and serving our neighbor that we come and give thanks go God. Every Sunday we hear about this sacrificial love in the Anaphora (offertory) prayers of the Divine Liturgy, "For God so loved the world as to give His only begotten Son, that whoever believes in Him may never perish, but have eternal life" (John 3:16).

We need to be reminded that loving other people is not optional; it is a command from Jesus Himself! One of the most sobering Gospel lessons in the New Testament is read on the Sunday of the Last Judgment, the Sunday before the beginning of Great Lent. The Gospel lesson is taken from Matthew 25 which is commonly called the Sheep and the Goats. Jesus teaches His disciples about the final judgment and tells them that when the Son of Man returns again all nations will be gathered before Him and He will separate them as a shepherd separates sheep from the goats. He will ask them whether they fed the hungry, clothed the naked, visited the sick and suffering, and welcomed the stranger. Those who did not serve and love the poor, will be sent to eternal punishment but the righteous to eternal life (Matthew 25:31–46). Thus, at the final judgment, we will be judged on one thing only: did we love the neighbor? Hopefully the answer will be a resounding yes!

This teaching about the last judgment pertains not only to individuals but to our missions and parishes as well. It is in the local worshipping community where we share our common Orthodox Faith and life and where we also have many opportunities to show love for the neighbor in very concrete and tangible ways. Our missions and parishes have a mandate to engage in outreach projects for the poor, orphan, hungry, naked, sick, and imprisoned. Engaging in outreach projects not only helps other people but it can also transform a parish community, especially as parishioners learn how to work together towards a common goal and sharing their times, talents, and treasures with other people in need. If we all look at the strengths and talents within our various parish communities I am sure that we can find countless ways to love and serve our neighbor, and in doing so, learning to love and serve the Lord.

CHAPTER THREE

THE HEALING OF THE WOMAN OF NAIN

(LUKE 7:11–16)

What shall we call you, O Apostle?
Heaven, for you have made an account of the glory of God for us?
Lightning, for you illumine the world with radiance?
A cloud, for you rain down in a torrent the knowledge of God?
A chalice pouring the rich wine of wisdom to gladden our hearts?
Pray to the Lord that He may save our souls!
(*Stikhera for Lord I Call Feast of St. Luke*)

The immediate context for today's Gospel lesson is found in the beginning of chapter seven, where Jesus heals the centurion's servant. A Roman centurion was a low-ranking official in the Roman military, but still maintained a level of social status in the larger community. We know from the Gospel that this particular centurion had a sick servant. The centurion came to Jesus asking Him to heal his servant. Jesus replied, "I tell you, not even in Israel have I found such faith" (Luke 7:9). As the man went home, he found that his slave had been healed.

Immediately following the healing story we have a story of the widow of Nain. Nain was a city in northern Palestine near the village of Nazareth, the village where Jesus lived. One day a widow from Nain was having a funeral for her dead son. In the ancient world a widow was considered the poorest of the poor. We have to remember that during the time of Jesus women had very little status in society and were largely supported by her husband, father, or eldest son. Luke tells us that this was her only son which meant that she was all alone and had no one to care for her. In other words, she is totally alone and among the lowest in the social order of the day (Acts 6:1–11 and 1 Timothy 5:3–16). As the funeral procession passed along, Jesus told the funeral bearers to stop and He told the young man, "Young man, I say to you, arise" (Luke 7:14). The young man arose and the Gospel says that the people made two important exclamations, "A great prophet has arisen among us" and "God has visited His people" (Luke 7:17).

In the Gospels, we see Jesus healing people, but only a few times does He raise someone from the dead. In John 11, Jesus raises His friend Lazarus from the dead. This is a very powerful miracle in that Lazarus was already dead four days before Jesus came to Bethany to see him. These miracles echo older stories in the Old Testament when Elijah raised the son of the Shunamite Woman:

> After this the son of the woman, the mistress of the house, became ill; and his illness was so severe that there was no breath left in him. And she said to Elijah, "What have you against me, O man of God? You have to come to me to bring my sin to remembrance, and to cause the death of my son!" And he said to her, "Give me your son." And he carried him up into the upper chamber, where he lodged, and laid him upon his own bed. And he cried to the Lord, "O Lord my God, hast thou brought calamity even upon the widow with whom I sojourn, by slaying her own son?" Then he stretched himself upon the child three times, and cried to the Lord, "O Lord my God, let this child's soul come into him again." And the Lord hearkened to the voice of Elijah; and the soul of the child came into him again, and he revived. And Elijah took the child, and brought him down from the upper chamber into the house, and delivered him to his mother; and Elijah said, "See, your son lives." And the woman said to Elijah, "Now I know that you are a man of God, and that the word of the Lord in your mouth is truth" (1 Kings 17:17–24. See also 2 Kings 4:32–37).

However, the real thrust of the passage is not the miracle, but the confession of faith that the miracle elicits from the crowd. At the end of the miracle story the crowd exclaims, "A great prophet has arisen among us" and "God has visited His people" (Luke 7:17).

In the Gospels, Jesus is often described as a prophet. In the Gospel of John when Jesus encounters the priests and Levites, they said to him, "Are you the prophet?" (John 1:21). When Jesus encountered the Samaritan woman and told her of her sinful behavior, she said to Him, "Sir, I perceive that You are a prophet" (John 4:19). During the Jewish feast of Passover, what we consider to be the entry into Jerusalem or Palm Sunday, the crowds were holding palm branches and leaves in honor of Jesus' triumphal entry. At one point the crowds exclaimed, "This is the prophet Jesus of Galilee" (Matthew 21:11).

By calling Jesus a prophet, people were identifying Him not only as a wise teacher or sage, but as someone who preached against the religious and cultural norms of society. The Old Testament prophets came preaching against the established religious leaders and customs because the Jewish leaders and kings were not being obedient to the Law of God. They were not taking care of the poor, the orphan, or the widow; they were neglecting to enforce real justice and equity. Thus, the Lord raised up prophets in order to remind people of the basics of God's love. Following religious customs and traditions was not enough, they had to be obedient to God alone and not worship idols, whether created by hand or in their creative imaginations. The God of the Scriptures is a jealous God who wants us to love and serve Him alone. Therefore, when people called Jesus a prophet, they were affirming his counter-establishment mindset as he continually questioned and challenged the religious customs that did not fall in line with God's righteousness and justice.

The prophets were also a sign that God was not an absent God that He was always with His people through His preached word. In other words, God first gave Israel a written Law through Moses but when Israel neglected to follow His Laws and commandments He sent them prophets in order to remind Israel about being obedient to Him. This shows God's care and concern for his people. At the end of today's Gospel lesson, the people proclaim that God has visited His people, which comes from another name for Jesus which is Emmanuel, which literally means God with us. He became one of us and experienced our pain, suffering, loss, grief, and joy. One of the hymns that we sing during the Vigil for the Nativity is "God is With Us," which is adapted from the Prophet Isaiah:

> The people who have sat in darkness have seen a great light; those who dwelt in the land of deep darkness on them has light shined. Thou hast multiplied a nation, Thou has increased its joy, they rejoice before Thee as with joy at the harvest, as men rejoice when they divide the spoil. For the yoke of his burden, and the staff of his shoulder, the rod of his oppressor, Thou hast broken as on the day of Midian. For every boot of the tramping warrior in battle tumult and every garment rolled in blood will be burned as fuel for the fire. For to us a son is given; and the government will be upon his shoulder, and his name will be called Wonderful Counselor, Mighty God, Everlasting Father, Prince of Peace.' And of the increase of his government and of peace there will be no end, upon the throne of David, and over his kingdom, to establish it, and uphold it with justice and righteousness from this time forth and forevermore. The zeal of the hosts will do this (Isaiah 9:2–7).

This long passage from Isaiah speaks about the Lord's messiah who will come and save us from darkness, despair, and utter destruction. The messiah will ultimately bring God's justice and righteousness to the earth, bringing equity among all peoples. Isaiah's words provide solace and comfort during times of great distress. Every generation has its wars, terror, fears, and doubts about the future. However, we cannot lose hope, knowing that our salvation is given to us by God Himself. We can never forget that.

CHAPTER FOUR

THE PARABLE OF THE SOWER

(LUKE 8:5–15)

How shall we address you, O chosen of God?
River, flowing forth to us from Paradise?
Ark of the covenant which Christ laid down?
Beacon, made radiant by spiritual light?
Lamp that enlightens the Church?
Bread of life, divine table, cup of spiritual drink
Pray to the Lord that He may save our souls!
(*Stikhera for Lord I Call Feast of St. Luke*)

Today we are presented with the fourth reading from the Gospel of Luke, which is the parable of the sower, a parable also found in Matthew 13:1–23 and Mark 4:1–20. When reading the Scriptures, we must keep in mind that Jesus used many images and metaphors that people would have understood during his time, especially the many agricultural images such as sowing and planting, harvesting, vines and vineyards, as well as sheep and shepherding. Jesus used metaphors as a way to get his point across to other people about the truth of God's love for us. When teaching about forgiveness, Jesus gave the example of the Prodigal Son. When He taught about unconditional love and being a neighbor, He used the parable of the Good Samaritan. When teaching about the Kingdom of Heaven, He used various images such as the image of the mustard seed or the king giving a grand banquet. Our task is to try to understand His teaching the best we can and learn how to read and understand these metaphors.

The parable of the sower speaks of the Gospel as a seed that is continuously being planted or sown. Jesus says that a sower went out and sowed his seeds. Some fell along the path and were trampled under foot, some fell on the rock and after it grew a little bit it withered away due to lack of water, some fell along the thorns which choked the seed, and finally some fell in the good soil and it yielded a large harvest, Luke says hundredfold.

According to Jesus, the seed is the word of God which is planted. The sower continues to sow his seed no matter where they may fall on the earth. In other words, the sower does not have control over where the seeds will fall nor does he control whether or not the seeds will grow. His job is only to sow, as we see in Paul's first epistle to the Corinthians, "I planted, Apollos watered, but God gave the growth. So neither he who plants nor he who waters is anything but only God who gives the growth. He who plants and he who waters are equal and each shall receive his wages according to his labor" (1 Corinthians 3:6–9). Paul was the first one to preach the Gospel to the Corinthians, Apollos followed Paul in his teaching and was the one who Paul says "watered" but ultimately God gave the growth of the Gospel as the Corinthian community continued to grow and increase. Paul had no control over the expansion of his communities, the growth of the Gospel depended solely on God alone.

The hope is that the seed, which is the Word of God, finds the good soil and takes root, grows, and provides and abundant harvest. The good soil is described of being a good and honest heart that accepts the word and allows it to flourish. In the Scriptures, the word heart is the very core or center of a person, the life force that keeps the body going. The head or brain was considered the rational or thinking aspect of a person but the heart was the center. Thus, if the heart was good and honest then the person could hear the Gospel and it will grow. If the heart is not honest, truthful, and open the Gospel will not grow. Furthermore, the Scriptures speak of two kinds of heart, a heart of stone, which is closed and a hard heart and a heart of flesh which is soft and pliable. When reading the Prophet Ezekiel, we see the descriptions of both a heart of stone and a heart of flesh:

Therefore say, "Thus says the Lord God: I will gather you from the peoples, and assemble you out of the countries where you have been scattered, and I will give you the land of Israel." And when they come there, they will remove from its detestable things and all its abominations. And I will give them one heart, and put a new spirit within their flesh and give them a heart of flesh, that they may walk in my statutes and keep my ordinances and obey them; and they shall be my people, and I will be their God. But as for those whose heart goes after their detestable things and their abominations, I will requite their deeds upon their own heads, says the Lord" (Ezekiel 11:17–21. See also Jeremiah 32:36–41).

God tells Ezekiel that He will give the Israelites one heart and that they will worship Him alone and turn away or repent from worshipping false idols. If someone has a divided heart, it means that they are not whole or complete, that their heart and mind is divided. However, the Lord wants Israel to have a single heart and that they will have a heart of flesh which is pliable, and thus, soft and open to repentance. The opposite of a heart of flesh is a heart of stone or hardened heart that is cold and unchangeable.

However, the goal of sowing seeds is not just to sow the seed but hopefully to reap a large harvest. No one plants a garden and expects a few vegetables and flowers. When planting a garden, we usually look forward to a huge crop of tomatoes, peppers, and cucumbers. No one plants a garden just to look at the nice green leaves. It is one thing to plant a garden but if a tomato plant does not bring forth tomatoes then what good is the plant? If my apple tree does not bring forth apples, what good is the apple tree? In other words, the hope is that the seeds produces fruit, and Luke states that it will produce a hundredfold.

When speaking about the harvest, the Apostle Paul speaks of bearing fruit which is the fruit of the Spirit, "but the fruit of the Spirit is love, joy, peace, patience, kindness, goodness, faithfulness, gentleness, self-control; against such there is no law" (Galatians 5:22). In his epistle to the Colossians, Paul also speaks in terms of the Gospel producing fruits as he commends the Colossians for their faith and commitment to Christ, "Of this you have heard before in the word of the truth, the Gospel which has come to you, as indeed the whole world it is bearing fruit and growing — so among yourselves, from the day you heard and understood the grace of God in truth" (Colossians 1:6) and "so that you may approve what is excellent, so that you may be pure and blameless for the day of Christ, filled with the fruits of righteousness which come through Jesus Christ, to the glory and praise of God" (Philippians 1:11). It is clear in both the Old and New Testaments that our vocation as Christians is to bear fruit.

The garden imagery that Jesus uses is a good one. When starting a garden, we have to prepare the soil, remove all the weeds, rocks, stones, and leaves that fell on the ground and accumulated during the autumn and winter months. Then we have to dig the soil and bring humus and other dead material in so that the soil will be good. We may bring some fertilizer to help the plants grow. Then we actually purchase the plants and seeds and plant the garden. Planting a garden is very hard work, and anyone who has done that knows the difficulty involved. However, we cannot have a good harvest if we do not take the time to prepare the soil and get everything ready.

Just as it is hard work planting and cultivating a garden so too is it hard work to hear the Gospel. Many people think that by just coming to Church and participating in the liturgical services that we can live a faithful life in Christ. Coming to Church services is only one part of the equation. We also have to make sure that our heart is open and prepared to hear the Word of God so that it finds soft ground in which it can be planted. Preparing our heart to hear the Gospel is no different than weeding a garden. If we want our flower or vegetable gardens to flourish, we have to rip out the weeds and the rocks, trim back the undergrowth, apply fresh mulch and humus, and keep the garden well drained and watered. In other words, preparing a garden takes a lot of work and effort. So does preparing our heart to hear the Word of God. There are many people who come to Church services but who are deaf to the Gospel and who refuse to truly repent and to follow Christ. However, the Church offers us various ways to help us prepare the "soil" of our heart: regular routines of prayer and fasting, participation in the sacrament of confession and holy communion, reading and reflecting on the lives of the saints, and regularly reading and studying the Scriptures. These various activities are not ends in themselves but are ways in which we prepare our heart to hear the Word and that it can blossom and bear fruits of repentance.

CHAPTER FIVE

THE RICH MAN AND LAZARUS
(LUKE 16:19–31)

What shall we call you, O God-inspired speaker?
A faithful steward of the mysteries of Christ?
A servant of the divine tent not made with human hands,
Perfected in the fullness of time by the Builder of wisdom?
He entrusted to you the new law of grace,
Inscribed in Zion on tablets hewn from the rock of love.
O faithful witness, pray to Him that our souls may be saved!
(*Stikhera for Lord I Call Feast of St. Luke*)

Jesus spent a lot of his life speaking about money and material things. We have many parables and teachings on money and how it relates to life: the parable of the Good Samaritan, the widow and the two coins, Jesus' chasing out the money changers from the Jerusalem Temple, and the parable of the Rich Man and Lazarus. This last parable inspired John Chrysostom, a bishop and pastor of the Church, to deliver numerous sermons just on this one parable! A selection from one of his sermons on the Rich Man and Lazarus is in the appendix in the back of the book for further reading and reflection.

In today's lesson we hear that an unnamed rich man was living lavishly in his large house while a poor man named Lazarus was begging outside his gates. It is interesting that Luke mentions that the rich man was unnamed while the poor man was named; it makes the poor man more human, more personal while the rich man seems very impersonal. We must keep in mind that this Lazarus is not the same Lazarus that we hear about in the Gospel of John. The name Lazarus is derived from the Hebrew word Eleazar, which means God has helped. We will see later in the story how God has helped the poor Lazarus.

The plot thickens as we hear of dogs licking Lazarus' wounds. In antiquity, dogs were considered dirty animals, and Luke says that these dirty and unclean animals actually took better care of Lazarus than did the rich man. The story takes a turn when both men die and Lazarus finds himself in heaven, or as Luke says, in Abraham's bosom. However, the rich man was in torments in Hades, which is the realm of the dead. In the Old Testament, Hades is also referred to as sheol, which is the place of death and darkness. If people were in Hades, it meant that they were dead and could no longer offer their praise and prayer to God.

The rich man begs Abraham to send Lazarus to refresh his anguish, yet Abraham refuses to fulfill his request. There is a great chasm or gulf between heaven and Hades. Then the rich man asks if Abraham would send Lazarus to his five brothers as a warning. Again, Abraham says no, they have Moses and the prophets and if they cannot believe what is written there, they will never believe a miracle of someone coming back from the dead (Luke 16: 31). This may seem like a harsh saying, one would think that the rich man is generally concerned about the welfare and future of his brothers. By sending Lazarus, he thinks that this will increase his brother's faith and commitment to the Lord and will change their ways. However, Jesus Himself says that if people cannot believe Moses and the things that are written about the messiah, they will certainly not listen to Him either, "If you believed Moses, you would believe Me, for he wrote of Me. But if you do not believe his writings, how will you believe My words?" (John 5:45–47).

People generally seek a sign or a miracle to increase their faith. Yet Luke is telling us something very important in today's reading. The Scriptures are the basis for our faith, miracles may occur now and then but our faith is not in the miracle, but in the teaching of the Gospel. The Apostle Paul reminds us that even a demon can come disguised as an angel of light. The second important lesson in today's reading is that the love of God is intimately connected with the love of the neighbor. Throughout the Scriptures God commands His people to love the poor, orphan, and widow because it is when we love our neighbor that we learn to love God:

Thus says the Lord: for three transgressions and for four, I will not revoke the punishment, because they sell the righteous for silver, and the needy for a pair of shoes-they trample the head of the poor into the dust of the earth, and turn aside the way of the afflicted (Amos 2:6–7).

When the son of man comes in His glory, and all the angels with Him, then He will sit on His glorious throne. Before Him will be gathered all the nations, and He will separate them from one another as a shepherd separates the sheep from the goats, and He will place the sheep at His right hand, but the goats on the left. Then the King will say to those at his right hand, "come o blessed of My Father, inherit the kingdom prepared for you from the foundation of the world; for I was hungry and you gave Me food, I was thirsty and you gave Me drink, I was a stranger and you welcomed Me, I was naked and you clothed Me, I was sick and you visited Me, I was in prison and you visited Me" (Matthew 25:31–36).

God is love. In this the love of God was made manifest among us, that God sent His only Son into the world, so that we might live through Him. In this is love, that we have loved God but that He loved us and sent His Son to be the expiation for our sins. Beloved, if God so loved us, we also ought to love on another (1 John 4:7–11).

As Christians we are called not just to hear and learn the Gospel but also to do it. The poor Lazarus was sitting by this man's gate day after day and the rich man chose not to see the reality that their was a poor and needy person who was literally at his feet begging for food. Yet the rich man chose not to help him. In the end it was too late since he was given an entire lifetime to perform acts of charity and love. We might think that Abraham's response to the rich man is cold, that he refuses to send Lazarus to his brothers or even to cool the tip of his tongue. Yet we know that there are some people will not believe even if they experience a great miracle! Luke's message is that we are called to love both God and neighbor now, if we put it off for tomorrow it will be too late.

CHAPTER SIX

CLEANSING OF THE DEMONIAC
(LUKE 8:26–39)

What shall we call you, O glorious one?
Treasury of heavenly gifts?
Steadfast physician of our souls and bodies?
Fellow-laborer of Paul and his companion in travel and hardship,
Who set down the Acts of the Apostles?
Luke, your exceeding goodness has won for you many names.
Pray to the Lord that He may save our souls!
(*Stikhera for Lord I Call Feast of St. Luke*)

Some scholars assume that demonic possession in the ancient world was attributed to mental illness, such as schizophrenia or other forms of mental illness. Many of the symptoms or manifestations of mental disorders may mimic what people think of demon possession; harming themselves or those people around them, speaking to someone who is not really there, or some other behavior. Modern medicine tells us that mental disorders can be treated with drugs and creates a sense of normal lifestyle for those people who are afflicted with such problems. However, while this may be true, we cannot discount demonic possession as a reality. Christians believe that Jesus Christ is the lord over all creation but we also know that evil exists in this world. The high rates of physical, emotional, and verbal abuse, warfare, terrorism, drug addiction, not to mention political corruption and other inhumane activities are evil actions and need to be named in order for us to properly fight against them.

Jesus was traveling in the area of the Gadarenes or in some translations we see the word Gergasenes. This area called Gadara is located approximately thirty-five miles south of the Sea of Galilee and was inhabited by many farmers and agricultural workers and also has a lot of large hills and mountains in the area. Gadarene was a city in eastern Palestine in the city of the Decapolis, which was an area of ten Roman Gentile cities which formed a loose political and social federation: Philadelphia, Raphana, Scythopolis, Gadara, Hippos, Dion, Pella, Gersa, and Canatha. All of these cities were on the eastern side of the Jordan River near the mountain range. This is perhaps why the text says that the demoniac used to live among the caves.

The man in the Gospel today was possessed by many demons for he told Jesus that his name was legion. In the Roman army a commander was in charge of a legion of men which was a group of one hundred soldiers. Therefore, this man was possessed by hundreds of demons. Apparently this man was a danger to himself and those around him since Luke tells us that he not only lived among the tombs but was also bound with chains and fetters. In antiquity, cemeteries were located outside of the city walls and were considered the realm of the dead and were often referred to as a necropolis or the city of the dead. People would visit the cemetery but we can imagine that it was a dismal place.

Furthermore, as we see throughout the Gospel of Luke and throughout the other Scriptures, it is the outsiders and the demons that know Jesus' true identity while His own disciples and His followers do not know Jesus' true identity. The demon-possessed man cried out with a loud voice, "What have you to do with me, Jesus, Son of the Most High God? I beseech You, do not torment me" (Luke 8:28). Jesus then drives out the demons and they run into the lake and they drowned. One would think that the townspeople would be happy because their friend was coherent and in his right mind again. However, their first reaction is anger, and they "asked Him to depart from them; for they were seized with great fear" (Luke 8:37). The townspeople responded out of anger towards Jesus because their main source of income was gone. In other words, these people placed greater emphasis on these pigs than on their friend.

The end of the lesson states that Jesus told the man to, "return to your home, and declare how much God has done for you" (Luke 8:39). The man went and followed Jesus' words. After this great miracle, this man becomes a type of apostle, someone who is sent out to proclaim the good news of the Gospel. He shares this good news since God healed him from his demon possession and now is in his right mind. The man who was broken and shattered is now made whole and complete.

CHAPTER SEVEN

THE HEALING OF JAIRUS' DAUGHTER AND THE WOMAN WITH THE FLOW OF BLOOD

(LUKE 8:41–56)

O Apostle of Christ,
Compiler of divine dogmas and foundation of the Church.
You were the attendant and imitator of Paul, the chosen vessel.
By wisdom you have rescued us from the turmoil of ignorance,
For our hearts were in the depths of destruction.
Therefore we beseech you:
"Most admirable Luke, the pride of Antioch,
Pray to our Savior and God,
For those who celebrate your most honorable memory in faith!"
(*Stikhera for Lord I Call Feast of St. Luke*)

Today's Gospel lesson immediately follows the story of Jesus driving out the demons into a herd of swine. Jesus is still in the Gentile area and while here encounters a ruler of the local synagogue named Jairus. While there was only one Temple based in the city of Jerusalem, there were many synagogues throughout the Roman Empire. The word synagogue means gathering together, and it is in the gathering where the Jews heard the Word of God and were instructed in the basic tenants of the Law and the Prophets. We know that both Jesus and the Apostle Paul often taught in the synagogue in the early part of their teaching ministry. Likewise, the ruler of the synagogue was responsible for the administrative duties of the religious community and was very influential among the people. This Gospel lesson is also found in both Matthew 9:18–26 and Mark 5:21–43.

Jairus came to Jesus because his only daughter was dying. Luke does not elaborate on the situation but one can assume that Jairus was quite distraught, after all, having to watch your child get sick and die is heart wrenching. Many mental health professionals say that having a child die is one of the worst things that people can go through in life. Not only was she his only daughter, but Luke tells us that she was twelve years old which means that she was almost an adult and that much time had passed with her parents.

This particular Gospel lesson is interesting because it contains a story within a story. The overall story of Jairus and his daughter serves as a frame for a shorter story of the woman suffering from a flow of blood for twelve years. Luke emphasizes that not only did she have a poor medical condition but that she sought out physicians who could not help her. Furthermore, according to the Jewish purity laws, this woman was considered to be unclean, yet she still managed to see out Jesus for help (Leviticus 15:25–30). So, in a spirit of desperation she did not even ask Jesus to heal her, but rather, "touched the fringe of his garment and immediately her flow of blood ceased" (Luke 8:44). She came to Jesus in faith knowing that even by touching the hem of His garment that she would be made whole again. Jesus tells her, "daughter, your faith has made you well, go in peace" (Luke 8:48).

Then the Jairus story is picked up again as a servant of Jairus' house comes to tell him that his daughter is now dead. Jesus, however, gives Jairus' and his friends hope by saying that if they have faith that she will be made well again. He then goes to Jairus' house and said to her, "Child arise" (Luke 8:34).

What should we make of these two stories? Well, perhaps these two miracles reinforce the fact that Jesus is the Lord over all creation and that all powers, even the power of Satan and the powers of sickness and death have no control over us, even in death. The story of Jairus' daughter is reminiscent of the raising of Lazarus found in the Gospel of John (John 11:1–44). Jesus' friend Lazarus died and was in the tomb for four days. Then his friends and family beg Jesus to come and to visit with them because they are in mourning. Jesus comes and not only visits with the family but raises Lazarus from the dead as a sign of His power even over death. Jesus tells Mary and Martha, "I am the resurrection and the life; he who believes in Me, though he die, yet shall he live, and whoever lives and believes in Me shall never die" (John 11:25).

Jesus is the lord over all creation. We see him calming the storms, driving out demons, healing people of their sickness, and even raising the dead. These miracles were not for entertainment purposes, but to show that He has power and authority over all things. This power is contrasted with the powers and principalities of this world such as sickness, war, and terrorism, which in the end have no real power over us.

CHAPTER EIGHT

THE PARABLE OF THE GOOD SAMARITAN
(LUKE 10:25–37)

With the net of charity, O admirable Luke,
You drew the human race from the sea of vanity,
And yielded them to the practice of the Master's commands.
As His apostle, He enlightened your understanding;
As His preacher, He revealed to you His incomprehensible Divinity, O
Most blessed one.
(*Litya Verse for Feast of St. Luke*)

The parable of the Good Samaritan is one of the most known of Jesus' parables and has been the inspiration for the naming of hospitals, charities, and other non-profit philanthropic organizations. Likewise when someone does a good deed, they are often referred to as being a good Samaritan.

This particular parable is found in the tenth chapter of Luke. In the beginning of the chapter, we see Jesus who sets His face against Jerusalem. In biblical language, to set ones face against something is akin to judgment. In other words, Jesus is going to Jerusalem to be judged, but in actuality it is Jesus, the Lord's anointed messiah who will pronounce His judgment against the powers and principalities of this world. As He begins His journey to Jerusalem, He encounters a lawyer who tests him about eternal life, "Teacher, what must I do to inherit eternal life?" This question seems strange since a lawyer would have presumably studied the Torah (Law) and knew very well what the words meant. However, the lawyers' question seems to be a leading question as a way to entice or entrap Jesus into a corner through the use of rhetoric. Jesus answers the lawyer by citing a passage from the Ten Commandments about loving both God and neighbor. However, the lawyer then pushes Jesus as he asks Him, "and who is my neighbor?" Again, it seems as if the lawyer wants to keep pushing Jesus into a corner. However, when we read the Gospels, we see that Jesus usually answers people with a question or a story. Jesus responds to the lawyer by using the parable of the Good Samaritan.

Jesus says that a man was traveling from Jerusalem to Jericho and fell among robbers. The narrow and rocky road from Jerusalem to Jericho was nearly 20 miles that went from 2,500 feet above seal level in Jerusalem to about 770 feet above seal level in Jericho, which is a very deep descent on treacherous paths. Jericho was one of the popular cities in the Old Testament; it was in Jericho where Joshua blew his horn and the walls of the city came tumbling down. Jericho was also in the vicinities of the tribes of Benjamin and Joseph two important tribes in the Old Testament. Furthermore, in the New Testament, Jericho is where Jesus heals the Bartimaeus and later visits Zachaeus who also lives in Jericho (Matthew 20:29 and Luke 19:1).

The parable says that three different people walked by the man on the side of the road, a priest and a Levite followed finally by a Samaritan. The priests and Levites were members of the religious elite in Judaism and hailed from the priestly lineage of Aaron. It was the Aaronic priesthood that established the Temple worship and who maintained the intricate rites, rituals, and ceremonies of the Temple. Luke does not tell us the exact reasons why both the priest and the Levite passed by the man alongside the road, but we can infer that since the man was bloody that they refused to have contact with him. It was against the Law to come into contact with anyone who was either unclean or if there was blood involved. Perhaps both the priest and Levite were late for a service in Jerusalem or had other errands to do and did not want to take the time to help someone.

Finally, a Samaritan came by and helped the man. This might not sound too impressive today but during the time of Jesus the Samaritans were considered religious and social outcasts. The Samaritans were a mixed race of Jews and pagans and lived in the area called

Samaria and were considered outcasts according to the Jews. Samaritans are mentioned at several intervals in the Scriptures; we have the famous story of Jesus and the Samaritan woman in the Gospel of John who was living in adultery as mentioned in John 4. Thus, to the hearers of the Gospel, this was a very strange thing that an outsider stopped to help this man while the two Jewish priests, members of the children of Israel, did not help him.

The story also mentions that the Samaritan used his own material and financial resources in order to help the hurt man, using his own oil and wine to help cauterize the wounds and then put him on his beast and brought him to an inn. In the ancient world oil and wine were not only used for food but also for medicinal purposes as well. Oil was a balm that helped soothe sores and wine was used as an antiseptic and it was used as a cleansing agent as we hear in the Book of Psalms, "and wine to gladden the heart of man and oil to make his face shine and bread to strengthen man's heart" (Psalm 104:15. See also Deuteronomy 28:40). Even today in the Orthodox liturgical rite of Holy Unction the priest anoints the sick person seven times with a small amount of oil mixed with wine as a symbol of healing and forgiveness of sins. We have evidence of this in the epistle to James, "Is anyone among you suffering? Let him pray. Is any cheerful? Let him sing praise. Is any among you sick? Let him call the elders of the church, and let them pray over him anointing him with oil in the name of our Lord; and the prayer of the faith will save the sick man, and the Lord will raise him up; and if he has committed sins, they will be forgiven. Therefore, confess your sins to one another, and pray for one another, that you may be healed" (James 5:13–15).

This parable is powerful as it shows us that love and compassion have no bounds. This Samaritan man took time out of his own day, at least an entire day to assist with this beaten and hurt person. He also used his own money, which was two days wages in order to assist the beaten and distraught person. We are reminded that we are called to do the same for other people. Jesus tells us that the entire Law and the Prophets can be reduced to one commandment, love of God and neighbor, "Hear, O Israel: the Lord our God is one Lord; and you shall love the Lord your God with all your heart, and with all your soul, and with all your might" (Deuteronomy 6:5). We fulfill one commandment by fulfilling the other, but both are needed. There is no limit to love just as there is no limit to forgiveness. At one point in the Gospels Jesus tells Peter that he is supposed to forgive seventy times seven which is the biblical way of saying an infinite amount of times. Likewise, the love for the other is beyond limits. We cannot make distinctions on whom we should love or how we should love, but that we simply love! If we can do this one thing perhaps we will have a chance to reach the heavenly Kingdom.

CHAPTER NINE

THE RICH FOOL

(LUKE 12:16–21)

In the form of fire the radiance of the Spirit descended on you.
He made you His chosen vessel.
Zealously you drove away the mist of godlessness
And enlightened the world with the mystery of faith by the wisdom of
Your words,
Most honorable Apostle Luke, eyewitness of Christ.
(*Litya Verse for Feast of St. Luke*)

The story of the rich fool comes between two very important Gospel lessons concerning money and material things. The passage immediately preceding this Gospel lesson states that a man in the crowd wanted Jesus to decide whether or not his brother should divide their families inheritance with the man. Jesus responded, "Man, who made me a judge or divider over you?" (Luke 12:14). Jesus then tells the crowd that they are to beware of all covetousness. Coveting means wanting something that is not ours. I may covet my neighbor's red corvette because I do not like my grey Saturn. I may covet a new suit or computer.

The other Scripture passage that immediately follows today's Gospel reading, is a lesson about not being anxious in life which has a parallel passage in the Gospel of Matthew (Matthew 6:25–33, 19–21). Here, Jesus tells his disciples that they are not supposed to be anxious about food, clothing, or their daily needs because everything that they need in life will be provided for them by the Lord, "Consider the lilies, how they grow, they neither toil nor spin, yet I tell you, even Solomon in all his glory was not arrayed like one of these." The passage ends with the statement, "For where your treasure is, there will your heart be also" (Luke 12:34).

These two passages serve as the larger context for today's reading which is rather short. Here we have a parable of an unnamed rich person. The parable has no other characters besides this rich man who Luke says, "brought forth plentifully." The parable states that this man had so many crops that he had nowhere to put them since his other barns were overflowing with crops. So he had big plans to build larger barns. But then Jesus tells us that one night God will say to him "Fool! This night your soul is required of you; and the things that you have prepared, whose will they be?"

The word fool is used throughout the Old Testament describing people who make poor choices in life and who do not take the wise advice of the elders. Very often the term fool is contrasted with wisdom or knowledge especially as we see in the Psalms and Proverbs:

> The fool says in his heart, "there is no God." They are corrupt, doing abominable iniquity; there is none that does good (Psalm 53:1).

> The wise son makes a glad father, but a foolish son is a sorrow to his mother. Treasures gained by wickedness do not profit, but righteousness delivers from death. The Lord does not let the righteous go hungry, but he thwarts the craving of the wicked (Proverbs 10:1–3).

> In everything a prudent man acts with knowledge, but a fool flaunts his folly (Proverbs 13:16).

> Wisdom builds her house but folly with her own hands tears it down (Proverbs 14:1).

> So I turned to consider wisdom and madness and folly; for what can the man who comes after the king? Only what he has already done. Then I saw that wisdom excels folly as light excels darkness. The wise man has his eyes in his head, but the fool walks in darkness, and yet I perceived that fate comes to all of them. Then I said to myself, "What befalls the fool will befall me also; why then have I been so wise? And I said to myself that this

is also vanity. For the wise man of the fool there is no enduring remembrance, seeing that in the days to come all will have been forgotten (Eccl. 2:12–16).

The fool is one who is not wise, who does not follow the Lord's direction and guidance. A fool thinks that they know everything, but they actually do not. So when Luke tell us that this man was a fool, it means that he was unwise, seeking to build bigger and bigger barns and not caring about the future which was his salvation. In other words, his priorities were out of balance and when the time came he was not ready.

This short parable is reminiscent of the parable of the ten virgins from the Gospel of Matthew that we hear during Holy Week. Jesus tells a parable about ten maidens who went to meet their bridegroom. Five were wise and took extra oil for their lamps. The other five were foolish and went to bed without taking extra oil. The bridegroom arrived very early in the morning while it was still dark. However, the five maidens did not have enough oil and when they asked to borrow oil from the wise virgins they said no. So the five foolish virgins had to go buy extra oil, however, the bridegroom came and the five wise maidens entered the bridal feast and the door was shut. When the five foolish maidens returned they could not go in. Matthew ends the parable by saying, "Watch therefore, for you know neither the day nor the hour" (Matthew 25:1–13. See also Mark 13). The main lesson here is that we are always to be prepared because we never know when the bridegroom (Jesus Christ) will return again and we must always be ready to meet him. In other words, we have to be on guard, be vigilant, and be prepared, unlike the fool in the parable who was busy building his barns in order to store his crops but at the same time was not vigilant over his soul. The real wealth in the gospel lesson is to relish in wisdom and knowledge which will get us father in life rather than being foolish.

CHAPTER TEN

THE HEALING OF THE INFIRM WOMAN
(LUKE 13:10–17)

With the lightning bolts of your preaching,
You enlightened those who sat in the darkness of ignorance, O glorious Luke.
Through faith, you revealed them to be the children of God the Master.
You loved Him through suffering and death
And so inherited His glory,
O wise, faithful, and inspired disciple.
(*Litya Verse for Feast of St. Luke*)

During the time of Jesus there was only one Temple and that was in Jerusalem. The first Temple was built by King Solomon as a religious and cultural center. The Scriptures provide us a lot of details regarding the size, shape, exterior, and interior of the Temple, but scholars are unsure as to the exact description since we have various descriptions of the Temple in the Old Testament. Needless to say, it was a rather large structure with many entrances and porticoes, large enough for a large gathering of people. However, the Temple was eventually destroyed and was rebuilt by King Herod, just prior to the birth of Jesus.

From the various descriptions that we have, the Temple complex must have been a very large structure and could hold many people. The Temple complex was not just a place for the Jews to worship but a place of social, cultural, and financial interactions. Due to the highly structured offering system, pilgrims would go to the Temple to purchase their grain and cereal offerings as well as livestock which would later be slaughtered. Jews would often make a pilgrimage to

Jerusalem during the holy days, especially during the Passover season in the springtime.

However, the Jews who did not live close to Jerusalem still gathered together for prayer, socializing, and interaction in the local synagogue. The word synagogue means gathering or coming together, and it was when the Jews gathered together for prayers and worship that they were a synagogue. The synagogue refers not so much to a building or physical structure but to the group of people who prayed together. There were many synagogues throughout the Mediterranean world. According to the Book of Acts, we know that the Gospel was first preached by the Apostle Paul when he traveled from synagogue to synagogue, preaching the death and resurrection of Jesus Christ. During Jesus' lifetime, we know that He too would often visit the local synagogue, proclaiming the good news of salvation (Luke 4:16–20).

Today's Gospel lesson begins by showing that Jesus was teaching in the local synagogue when an infirm woman came to Jesus. Not only was she sick, but she had a bone problem that caused a bent back for eighteen years. We do not know any other details about this woman other than that she was infirm and that Jesus healed her.

The Jewish leaders were upset at Jesus because he healed her on the Sabbath. According to the Jewish Law, the Sabbath was considered to be a holy day and no work was to be done, honoring the story in Genesis when we hear that God created for six days, but on the seventh day He rested from His work, "Thus the heavens and the earth were finished, and all the host of them. And on the seventh day God finished His work which He had done, and He rested on the seventh day from all His work that He had done. So God blessed the seventh day and hallowed it, because on it God rested from all His work which He had done in creation" (Genesis 2:1–3). Later in the Book of Exodus we have further mention of the importance of the Sabbath in the life of Israel, "You shall keep the Sabbath, because it is holy for you; every one who profanes it shall be put to death; whoever does any work on it, that soul shall be cut off from among his people" (Exodus 31:14).

Yet we see Jesus going against the common understanding of the Sabbath in order to do a greater good. He asks the Jews, what is more important, to have the woman remain bent over and cripple or to heal her? He says to them, "Does not each of you on the Sabbath untie his ox or his ass from the manger, and lead it to water it? And ought not this woman, a daughter of Abraham whom Satan bound for eighteen years, be loosed from this bond on the Sabbath day?" (Luke 13:15–16).

Jesus is not afraid to question and even rebel against the common religious and social customs of His time in order to teach a greater lesson. While it was a common practice to observe the Sabbath in a strict manner, it was better to heal this woman and make her whole again. In other passages in the New Testament, Jesus says that the Sabbath was made for man not man for the Sabbath. Jesus restores this woman back to health but also back to the community, she is no longer in pain. We see Jesus as the source of true power and authority over all creation, even over sickness and death.

This story tells us a few things. First and foremost it is a story about love since Jesus went out of His way to heal this woman. Second, that Jesus truly goes against the common religious values of His day in order to teach the people about the true meaning of God's Word. In other words, Jesus was acting prophetically, very much like the prophets in the Old Testament. All of the prophets went against the common social, cultural, and religious values of their day in order to show how God is working in the world. When the Israelites fixated on the liturgical rites and rituals surrounding the Temple the prophets said that the Lord requires mercy and not sacrifice. The prophets preached the good news of salvation which goes against the *status quo*, especially in response to the lack of care for the poor, orphans, widows, and the destitute. We would do well to really pay attention to the Gospel lesson today because we can learn a lesson about our role in the Church. It is very easy to get wrapped up in the liturgical rites and rituals and ignore the other areas of life such as helping and serving the poor and the needy. This does not mean that one is opposed to the other but that both are needed in our obedience to Christ and the Gospel. The way to repentance is through actively serving the needy neighbor who is anyone who comes into our life. The problem is that when we get so enraptured by the liturgical life that we forget about acts of service and mercy. Again, we need to keep in mind that the Lord requires not sacrifice but mercy. May we always show mercy upon our neighbor through concrete acts of love in order to appropriately worship the Lord.

CHAPTER ELEVEN

THE RICH RULER
(Luke 18:18–27)

You forsook earthly things and followed after Christ.
You were signed with the inspiration of the Holy Spirit
And sent by Him to the nations, which were perishing,
To turn men to the light of the knowledge of God.
Having completed the struggles, O Apostle Luke,
Of your divine suffering and many torments,
You surrendered your soul into the hands of Christ.
Entreat Him, O most blessed one,
That He may grant us great mercy!
(*Litya Verse for Feast of St. Luke*)

Throughout the Gospels, we see that the Jewish leaders attempt to trap Jesus in His words. They gather together in order to make a spectacle of Him and embarrass Him among His friends. Today we see such an encounter with the story of the rich ruler.

This unnamed rich ruler comes to Jesus asking Him what he needs to in order to inherit eternal life. This question immediately follows after Jesus tells the crowd that whoever receives a child is actually receiving the Kingdom of God, "Truly, I say to you, whoever does not receive the kingdom of God like a child shall not enter it" (Luke 18:17). To be like a child is to be totally open to God's will and to be thankful for everything. Being like a child also means to be totally dependant upon the parents since children cannot do things for themselves. Young children need to be fed and nourished, have their diapers changed, comforted when they cry, and so forth. In other words, children are totally dependent on their parents for everything.

We are supposed to be like children in relation to God, being dependant on Him in our life.

The rich ruler comes asking Jesus a very important question, somehow he thinks that he can do something within his power to achieve the kingdom. Being wealthy puts him in this frame of mind since those with wealth are used to getting their way in life. However, after Jesus tells him that he has to follow the commandments in the Old Testament, he ends with a strong statement, "Sell all that you have and distribute to the poor, and you will have treasure in heaven; and come follow me" (Luke 18:22). The man goes away sorrowful because he has great possessions.

Then Jesus mentions that it is easier for a camel to go through the eye of the needle than for a rich man to enter into the Kingdom of Heaven. The eye of a needle has a double meaning. On the one hand it refers to an impossibility; how can a camel go through an eye of a needle; a camel is very large animal while a needle is very small. However, commentators refer to the "eye of a needle" as one of the gates in Jerusalem. Jerusalem had many gates which allowed people to enter and exit the city. One of the gates was called the "eye of a needle," which refers to a very narrow gate. In other words, a camel which was a beast of burden could not enter through the gate if the camel was weighed down with goods. Jesus tells the man, and us, a very important lesson. We need to enter the kingdom bare, with nothing since eternal life is a gift that is granted unto us. In other words we cannot earn our entrance into eternal life, there is nothing that we can do to achieve it, it is a gift of grace that is granted to us. Very often we think that our prayers, almsgiving, charitable work, or other good works somehow earns us good points with God and that He will bless us with eternal life. However, this is faulty thinking. The good works that we do should flows from our faith and commitment to God. If we remain faithful to the Lord and to the Gospel we will want to share this by doing good works in the world. Yet, God's salvation is always granted as a pure gift of grace and cannot be purchased or earned by human standards.

CHAPTER TWELVE

CLEANSING OF THE TEN LEPERS
(LUKE 17:12–19)

Grace is poured out upon your lips like a tongue of fire:
You received the word of light, O Apostle Luke.
You proclaimed salvation for those who longed to be made children of light,
Writing and teaching the holy Gospel in the fragrance of truth,
Compiling faithfully the deeds and words of Paul, your teacher.
Your holy writings are powerful weapons of light!
Through them we pierce the darkness of evil.
Pray that we may love the Light of all,
That, delivered from the corruption of death,
We may be granted peace, eternal light and great mercy!
(*Apostikha for Feast of St. Luke*)

In the ancient world leprosy was considered a grave disease. Leprosy was a cause for someone to be shunned from the community since leprosy was a highly contagious disease and eventually caused death. Lepers were considered unclean and were banished from the local community because they might spread their disease. Of all the diseases and maladies during the time of Jesus, leprosy was considered among the worst. We have some details regarding detecting leprosy in the Book of Leviticus:

> But if there is on the bald head or the bald forehead a reddish-white diseased spot, it is leprosy breaking out on his bald head or his bald forehead. Then the priest shall examine him, and if the diseased swelling is reddish-white on his bald head or on his bald forehead, like the appearance of leprosy in the skin of the body he is a leprous man, he is unclean; the priest must pro-

nounce him unclean; his disease is on his head. The leper who
has the disease shall wear torn clothes and let the hair of his
head hang loose, and he shall cover his upper lip and cry, "unclean, unclean." He shall remain unclean as long as he has the
disease; he is unclean: he shall dwell alone in the habitation of
the camp (Leviticus 13:42–46).

The text continues at great length discussing the types of clothes
that the leper has to wear as well as the various examinations that
have to be undertaken by the priest. Apparently leprosy was a disease
that required extreme measures as to not contaminate the rest of the
community.

Ten lepers approached Jesus saying, "Jesus, master, have mercy on
us" (Luke 17:13). Again, we see that it is the outsiders, the lepers, the
demons, the Samaritans and Gentiles who seem to know Jesus' true
identity while the Jews, the chosen people of Abraham, do not seem
to know Jesus' identity or understand why Jesus is doing all of these
miracles and preaching the Gospel. Yet these ten lepers seem to know
Jesus' true identity as their master and Lord. After Jesus tells them to
go to the priests, they presumably go, but out of the group of ten only
one returns (Leviticus 13:2–3, 14:2–32). Luke tells us that not only did
one of the lepers return but that he was both a leper and a Samaritan.
In other words, he was considered a double outcast. There was no way
one could get farther from the chosen people of God then being both
a Samaritan and afflicted with the disease of leprosy!

This man had enough guts, determination, and faith to return
back to Jesus and give Him praise. Jesus tells him, "Rise and go your
way; your faith has made you well" (Luke 17:19). The man's deep faith
was the only thing required or expected of the man a sentiment which
is also highlighted throughout the Scriptures. In the Gospel of Matthew, we encounter a woman who touched Jesus' garment because
she was hemorrhaging for many years. After she touched the hem of
His garment, Jesus said, "Take heart, daughter, you faith has made
you well. And instantly the woman was well" (Matthew 9:22. See also
Mark 5:34 and Luke 8:48). In the Gospel of Luke, Jesus healed a blind

man who said, "Lord, let me receive my sight." And Jesus said to him, "Receive your sight: your faith has made you well. And immediately he received his sight and followed Him, glorifying God; and all the people, when they saw it, gave praise to God" (Luke 18:41–43). The result of the lepers' faith and of the woman with the flow of blood is that they were not only healed by they praised God, the result of their faith. When we have strong faith, we bless God for His love, mercy, and compassion on us. In other words, we offer God thanksgiving or gratitude for the abundance of gifts that He has bestowed upon us.

This sense of gratitude and thanksgiving is expressed in our weekly Eucharist service called the Divine Liturgy. Every Sunday we gather together as the Church of God to give thanks for everything that He has given us. We give thanks for the creation, for our leaders, for our spiritual guides, and most importantly for His only-begotten Son Jesus Christ as we hear in the prayers of the Liturgy:

> Thou it was who brought us from non-existence into being, and when we had fallen away didst raise us up again, and didst not cease to do all things until Thou hadst brought us up to heaven, and hadst endowed us with Thy Kingdom which is to come. For all these things we give thanks to Thee, and to Thine only begotten Son, and to Thy Holy Spirit" and later on we hear the following prayer, "We give thanks unto Thee, O King invisible, who by Thy measureless power didst make all things, and in the greatness of Thy mercy didst bring all things from non-existence into being.

We can sum up the entire liturgy on Sunday as a thanksgiving to God for everything that He has done for us. It is this spirit of gratitude and generosity that we are called to foster and cultivate in our life together as the living and growing body of Christ, fed and nourished on His Word and on His body and blood. However, so often we focus on what we do not have, rather than the many blessings that we do have. The Lord has truly provided us with so much, perhaps we can take time out of our day to offer our gratitude to Him.

CHAPTER THIRTEEN

THE GREAT BANQUET
(LUKE 14:16–24)

You beheld the fullness of God's mysteries;
Your words are a sure fortress of faith.
To you was entrusted the task of writing the Word of Life for us.
You faithfully obeyed God's inspiration,
Eyewitness and minister of the incarnate Word;
You beheld Him after the Resurrection together with Cleopas,
Recognizing Him with hearts aflame in the breaking of bread.
Pray that He may fill the souls of all who keep your holy memory,
With the sweetness of divine fervor!
(*Apostikha for Feast of St. Luke*)

In the ancient world meals were considered more than just culinary activities and gastronomic events. They served as a forum for social and communal interaction. Meals lasted quite a long time as people gathered together sharing a meal and discussing the past days events or making business plans for tomorrow. This is idea of sharing a meal is much different than our modern fast food understanding of meals such as eating burgers and fries in the car during lunch break or on the way home from work. The ancients were not familiar with microwaveable meals or TV dinners. For them, eating together was considered a communal event where they shared intimacy and community.

Understanding the importance of meals in antiquity also provides for us a better understanding of the Gospel. The Evangelists tell us that Jesus spent a lot of His time eating with people, usually the ones who were social outcasts and sinners. Last week we read that Jesus had din-

ner with Zacheaus the tax collector. We also know that Jesus both host-
ed and attended meals Himself, He was present at the wedding feast
in Cana of Galilee where He changed water into wine, He fed the five
thousand with loaves of bread and fish, He ate the Passover meal with
His disciples, and after the resurrection He even ate honeycombs and
fish on the shore with His disciples. Today we hear Jesus teaching the
people by using a parable about a rich man hosting a grand banquet.

A rich man gave a banquet and invited many people. However, for several reasons people turned down the invitation: someone
bought a field and had to go see it, another bought some oxen and
had to tend to them, and another went out and got married and had
to take of his wife. When the man heard this, he sent out his servant
to the "highways and hedges" and compelled people to come in. The
parable ends emphatically, "For I tell you, none of those men who
were invited shall taste my banquet" (Luke 14:24). A similar passage
is found in Matthew 8:11, "I tell you, many will come from east and
west and sit at my table with Abraham, Isaac, and Jacob in the kingdom will be thrown into the outer darkness; there men will weep and
gnash their teeth."

The passage from Matthew refers to the great messianic banquet.
The phrase, the children of Abraham, Isaac, and Jacob refers to the
children of the promise who are the children of Israel. However, we
know that the Gospel was preached not just to Israel, God's chosen
people, but also to the Gentiles. Thus, while the sons of the kingdom
will be thrown out, those among the nations will accept the invitation
and will be invited to the banquet.

The kingdom of Heaven is often referred to as a banquet which
we see in several key passages of Scripture:

> On this mountain the Lord of hosts will make for all peoples a
> feast of fat things, a feast of wine on the lees, of fat things full of
> marrow, of wine on the lees well refined. And He will destroy
> this mountain the covering that is cast over all peoples, the veil
> that is spread over all nations. He will swallow up death forever,
> and the Lord God will wipe away tears from all faces, and the

reproach of his people he will take away from the earth; for the Lord has spoken (Isaiah 25:6–8).

And as they were eating, He took bread, and blessed, and broke it, and gave it to them, and said, "Take, this is My body." And He took a cup, and when He had given thanks He gave it to them and they all drank of it. And He said to them, "This is My blood of the covenant, which is poured out for many. Truly, I say to you, I shall not drink again of the fruit of the vine until that day when I drink it new in the Kingdom of God" (Mark 14:22–25).

Then the kingdom of heaven shall be compared to ten maidens who took their lamps and went to meet the bridegroom. Five of them were foolish and five were wise. For when the foolish took their lamps, they took no oil with them; but the wise took flasks of oil with their lamps. As the bridegroom was delayed, they all slumbered and slept. But at midnight there was a cry, "Behold, the bridegroom! Come out to meet him." Then all those maidens rose and trimmed their lamps. And the foolish said to the wise, "Give us some of your oil, for our lamps are going out." But the wise replied, "Perhaps there will not be enough for us and for you; go rather to the dealers and buy for themselves." And while they went to buy, the bridegroom came, and those who were ready went in with him to the marriage feast; and the door was shut. Afterward the other maidens came also, saying, "Lord, Lord, open to us." But He replied, "Truly, I say to you, I do not know you." Watch therefore, for you know neither the day nor the hour" (Matthew 26:1–13).

Then I heard what seemed to be the voice of a great multitude like the sound of many waters and like the sound of mighty thunder peals, crying, "Hallelujah! For the Lord our God the Almighty reigns. Let us rejoice and exult and give Him the glory, for the marriage of the Lamb has come, and His Bride has made herself ready; it was granted her to be clothed with fine linen, bright and pure" for the fine linen is the righteous deeds of the saints (Revelation 19:6–9).

Additional passages such as these are found throughout the Scriptures. All of them point to the future banquet that we will enjoy for eternity. However, our time together now is a preparation for that eternal meal. In other words, every time that we gather together for the Eucharist during the Divine Liturgy we are in a way preparing ourselves how to live and act now as if we were already in the Kingdom of God. Thus, we are constantly faced with the fact that Jesus has invited sinners, prostitutes, beggars, and the poor to His banquet, and as a priest once said to me, there will be many surprises which await us on the other side of the pearly gates of heaven! If we are not careful now, might find ourselves, like the five foolish virgins, watching the great feast from the purview of the front door rather than from inside, enjoying the master's hospitality!

Perhaps then this Gospel is a much-needed wake up call for repentance. While we are still alive we are given this time to love God with all of our heart, soul, mind, and strength, and our neighbor. We also can be involved in charity and outreach to those who are less fortunate. Time is short, as the passage from Matthew says, and we will neither know the time nor the hour when the Bridegroom will return. Hopefully He will find us ready and waiting for Him and we will enter the great marriage supper of the Lamb where we will behold the glory of the Lord and cry with all of the saints, "Hallelujah!"

CHAPTER FOURTEEN

ZACHAEUS

(LUKE 19:1-10)

Rejoice, blameless writer of the Gospel of joy;
You have recorded for us the conception and preaching of the Baptist;
The wondrous Annunciation to the Mother of the Lord;
The ineffable Incarnation and Birth of the Word Who came forth from
her womb;
His temptations, miracles and parables,
His Passion, Cross and death,
The glory of His risen body recognized in the breaking of bread,
His glorious Ascension and the coming of the Holy Spirit.
As a faithful witness you compiled the Acts of the Apostles.
You were Paul's companion in travel and his greatest consolation,
Beholder of divine mysteries and light of the Church.
Guard us all, O glorious healer!
(*Apostikha Verse for Feast of St. Luke*)

Before we fully enter into Great Lent, we encounter five preparatory Sundays which include the Sunday of Zachaeus, the Publican and the Pharisee, the Prodigal Son, the Last Judgment (Meat-
fare), and Forgiveness Sunday (Cheesefare). I always remembered
that Lent would soon be around the corner when I heard about Zachaeus climbing up the sycamore tree. With the Sunday of Zachaeus we
know that there is no turning back now, the Church has started the
cycle of readings that prepare us for the long journey that awaits us.
The Church slowly walks us through some important Gospel readings that speak of repentance, prayer, and love. Each Gospel story is
another step closer to the great fast which has been called a "school of
repentance." The first three preparatory Sunday's include Gospel les-

sons from the Gospel of Luke while the remaining two Sunday's have
readings from Matthew; Matthew 25:31–46 and Matthew 6:14–21 re-
spectively. Since the first three preparatory Sunday's include readings
from the Gospel of Luke they are included in this book.[1]

The Gospel lesson tells us that as Jesus entered Jericho, He encountered a man named Zachaeus and Luke tells us that he was no
ordinary man but a chief tax collector who was very rich. We also
know that Levi was also a tax collector but as soon as he met Jesus, he
left his tax booth and followed Jesus. His name was later changed from
Levi to Matthew and was one of Jesus' disciples. Tradition says that
he authored the Gospel of Matthew. These are the only two passages
where we are told that Jesus encountered a chief tax collector.

In antiquity, the Roman government levied various types of taxes
on the people in the empire in order to generate revenue. Many of
these tax collectors served as sub-contractors, they would collect the
tax for the Romans, but they would also include a high commission
in order to bolster their meager salary. Furthermore, we are not told
directly about Zachaeus' pedigree, but since he has a Jewish name, it
is most likely that he was a Jew. Thus, Zachaeus was a Jew working
for the Roman Empire which to the eyes of many Jewish people was
an outrage. We need to keep in mind that the Roman Empire was in
full control over the entire area and Zachaeus was probably seen as
a traitor or at least collaborating with the enemy, very similar to the
Vichy government in France during World War II that collaborated
with the Nazi government.

Zachaeus wanted to see Jesus, but got more than he bargained
for since Jesus told him that he wanted to come to his house. This
was more than a dinner invitation. To be invited to someone's house
meant that they wanted to share fellowship with that person. In other
words Jesus overlooked the fact that he was a tax collector and want-

---

[1] There are excellent resources on the themes and liturgical rites of Great Lent,
especially Thomas Hopko, *The Lenten Spring* (Crestwood, NY: St. Vladimir's
Seminary Press, 1998) and *Great Lent: Journey to Pascha* (Crestwood, NY: St.
Vladimir's Seminary Press, 1969).

ed to go visit with him. Jesus' comment instilled anger in the crowd as they said, "He has gone in to be the guest of a man who is a sinner" (Luke 19:7). This passage which is very similar to an earlier verse where Jesus calls Levi who also happens to be a tax collector:

> After this He went out, and saw a tax collector, named Levi, sitting at the tax office; and He said to him, "Follow me." And He left everything and rose and followed Him. And Levi made Him a great feast in his house; and there was a large company of tax collectors and others sitting at table with them. And the Pharisees and their scribes murmured against the disciples, saying, "Why do you eat and drink with tax collectors and sinners?" and Jesus answered them, "Those who are well have no need of a physician, but those who are sick; I have not come to call the righteous, but sinner to repentance" (Luke 5:27–32).

The last line in this passage is the most revealing: that Jesus came to heal the sick (the sinners) and not those who are well. Our Divine Liturgy contains a line in the prayer after the Lord's Prayer where the priest says, "Heal the sick, O Thou who art the physician of our souls and bodies." Jesus is the great Physician who comes and heals us, who cleanses our sins and heals our spiritual wounds and maladies. However, Jesus does not force His way into our life, but as with Zachaeus, He invites us to come over our house, to dwell and be with us.

Furthermore, the true healing comes through the preaching of the Gospel, for it is the proclamation of the good news of Jesus Christ that restores our relationship or communion with God. When we hear the Gospel, we should realize that we are sinners, and as the Apostle Paul says, of whom I am the first. Then, we confess our sins to God, repenting of our evil ways, and living a Christ centered life following His commandments to the narrow way of the Kingdom. The power of the Gospel is clearly seen in the Sacrament of Holy Unction. While the priest anoints the sick person with oil and wine, he first reads a series of seven epistle readings and seven Gospel readings before anointing the sick person at the end of the service. Then at the conclusion of the service the priest places the open Gospel book upside down upon the head of the sick person as he reads the prayer for forgiveness of sins. This is such a powerful image. The Gospel, literally the good news, is poured over the sick person which hopefully produces healing and comfort during their illness. The fourth century pastor and bishop John Chrysostom uses this image of the physician when he describes the work and ministry of the pastor. He says that the pastor is like a physician and rather than using bandages and medicines the priest only has the power of the Word which heals, binds, and soothes peoples pains. Today we are called to put our burdens on the Lord so that he can sustain and heal us of our pains, hurts, and maladies and that we, like Zachaeus, can find our salvation with Christ the Lord.

CHAPTER FIFTEEN

THE PUBLICAN AND THE PHARISEE
(LUKE 18:10–14)

All-wise Apostle,
Faithful laborer of the Savior,
Witness of the triumph of His Passion,
You have completed the race, you have kept the faith,
Harvesting the peoples from the darkness of error,
Offering us as a sweet-smelling oblation to the heavenly King.
Now you stand before the Judge of all;
Pray that He may rescue us from our sins
And deliver us from eternal death,
When He comes in glory on the Day of Judgment.
(*Apostikha Verse for Feast of St. Luke*)

The second preparatory Sunday includes the Gospel reading about the publican and the Pharisee. A publican is another word for tax collector. Here we have another Gospel reading about tax collectors as well as the Pharisee who was among the Jewish leaders during the time of Jesus. The Pharisees were the educated elite and were the interpreters of the Law.

Here we have a tax collector and the Pharisee both in the Temple praying to God. The Pharisee offered a prayer that was very self-centered, enumerating his good qualities boasting of what things he has done in his life. There is no offering of contrition or any sign of remorse or repentance for pain or suffering that he has inflicted on others. Then the publican prays in a very sincere and open manner, standing far away from the Pharisee and beating his breast saying, "God, be merciful to me a sinner." Jesus ends this short parable with a simple phrase, "for every one who exalts himself will be humbled, but he who humbles himself will be exalted" (Luke 18:14).

The message in the parable is Jesus injunction about humility. The publican prayed in a humble way, simply acknowledging his sinfulness without making excuses or rationalizations about what he has done, not heaping up long prayers but in a contrite and simple manner, God be merciful to me a sinner. The publican offered the more acceptable prayer than did the Pharisee and as Jesus says, was justified.

Jesus came preaching a Gospel of humility. His preaching stirred up the traditional cultural, religious, and social norms of his day. He spent time with harlots, publicans, Samaritans, lepers, as well as adulterers and Gentiles. In other words, he did what most people would not do and that is to reach out to those on the margins of society and welcome them to God's house bringing his saving message to anyone who had ears to hear. Meanwhile the children of Abraham, God's chosen people, seemed to have hardened hearts and stiff necks and did not want to hear the good news. Yet Jesus kept on preaching this good news until His very last breath. It was for the sick that He came, not the healthy.

Today's reading shows a very healthy person, the Pharisee, who has no need for healing, while the publican asks for God's forgiveness. This short prayer of the Publican has also come down to us in the form of the Jesus Prayer which has various forms. The conventional way that it is said it, "O Lord, Jesus Christ, Son of God, have mercy on me a sinner." The Jesus Prayer can be said basically anytime and anywhere, on the way to work, while working in the yard, while taking a walk, while taking a shower, or when doing housework or other chores. The prayer was originally practiced by the monks in the Egyptian desert as a way to always keep the Lord on their mind and on their lips, following Paul's command to pray ceaselessly (1 Thessalonians). The Jesus Prayer is a continual reminder that we are indeed sinners but that our only Lord and Master is Jesus Himself, and as the Apostle Paul says, that every knee and heaven on earth and in the regions under the earth will bow (Philippians 2). Jesus is our physician of souls and bodies, and He offers His saving hand to us if we want it. It is in through simple confession of sins and motivation to change that we have a chance at a new life, as we saw previously in the story of Zachaeus and now with the parable of the Publican and the Pharisee.

CHAPTER SIXTEEN

THE PRODIGAL SON
(LUKE 15:11–32)

Holy Apostle and Evangelist Luke,
Entreat the merciful God
To grant our souls forgiveness of transgressions.
(*Another Troparion for the Feast of St. Luke*)

Today we come to the final reading from Luke before entering into the season of Great Lent. The context for the reading is revealed in the opening verses of the chapter, "Now tax collectors and sinners were all drawing near to hear Him. And the Pharisees and the scribes murmured, saying, 'This man receives sinners and eats with them'" (Luke 15:1–2). Throughout the Gospel of Luke we have seen how Jesus goes out of His way to those on the margins of society, to the blind and the lame, the demon possessed, those who are ritually impure, and to the Gentile Roman soldiers. As we saw previously with the person of Zachaeus, Jesus even offers His hand of hospitality to the tax collectors and government workers. Jesus breaks all social, religious, and political mores and expectations in order to show that He is bringing a prophetic word which is the Gospel of salvation. This Gospel is one that changes and alters our common thinking and understanding.

Luke tells us that a man had two sons and one of these sons asked for his inheritance. This might seem like a normal request, however, we also have to remember that in antiquity the eldest son inherited everything. Yet already we see something different happening, the father concedes and gives the youngest son his portion. The youngest son also leaves and goes off into a far country while the eldest son remains with the father.

The story continues with some important details. The youngest son squandered his possessions in loose living. He also found himself in hunger and want since a famine arose in that country. In order to survive, the young man had to live amongst Gentile outsiders since Luke says that his job was feeding pigs. Jewish purity laws forbade them to deal with pork products, and we can infer that these people were either Gentiles or non-law abiding Jews. In any case he seemed to hit bottom. He left his father and home, lost all his possessions, was hungry, and had to feed the pigs.

However the young boy wanted to return home and made up a speech that he was going to tell his father. Yet, as he was returning to his father, the father ran out and welcomed his son home. The father did not ask questions, did not accuse his son of wasting his time and money, and did not say, "I told you so." Rather, the father immediately told his servants to prepare a celebration for his son. The story does not end there. All the while, the eldest son who never left the father was upset that the father was making such a big celebration for his other son. In other words, he was jealous that the father never game him a party. The father responded to the son by saying, "Son, you are always with me, and all that is mine is yours. It was fitting to make merry and be glad, for this your brother was dead, and is alive; he was lost, and is found" (Luke 15:31–32), which is repeated earlier in Luke 15:24. Just as the father in this story forgave and welcomed back his son, so too, does the Lord welcome us back as well.

I have always found this story to be very comforting. That no matter how far I seem to stray from the narrow path, following my own selfish desires, the Lord is always there running out to welcome me. This is very humbling experience, knowing that no matter how far we go away, no matter what we do, we are welcomed back, with open arms, with God's never ending mercy, compassion, and forgiveness which is seen in the prayer of confession:

O God our Savior, who through Thy prophet Nathan have granted to the penitent David forgiveness of his sins, and have received Manasseh's prayers of repentance, in Thy loving-kindness receive us Thy servants who repent of all the sins we have committed, and overlook all that we have done, O Thou who forgive offences and pass over transgressions. For Thou, O Lord, have said that You do not desire the death of a sinner but that he should turn from his wickedness and live! And that sins should be forgiven even unto seventy times seven. How beyond compare is Thy greatness, and Thy mercy is without measure, for if Thou should regard iniquity, no-one could stand. For Thou are the God of the penitent and to Thou we ascribe glory, to the Father, and to the Son, and to the Holy Spirit, now and ever and unto ages of ages. Amen.

This theme of reconciliation and forgiveness is expressed so beautifully in the Sacrament of Confession. When we go to confession to our priest, we go with a spirit of humility, confessing our sins to the priest. Like the younger son in the parable, we have wasted so much of our time, talents, and treasure on loose living very often following our own hearts' desire rather than following the Lord. Not only do we come confessing our sins but we also seek advice from our priest, who like us, is also a sinner. Our priest will try to direct us back on the narrow way to the Kingdom, focusing our attention on the one needful thing which is being obedient to Christ in our life. Hopefully we leave confession with a clean heart, seeking once again to serve both God and neighbor in our life. When we fall again, we will be welcomed back with open arms, once again, receiving the mercy, love, and compassion of God.

Throughout our journey we have heard of many miracles and teachings from Jesus. We know that Luke speaks of Jesus as the great savior of the world, the Lord's messiah who brings the Gospel to the whole world, and as the title of this book states, to the Gentiles or nations. In many ways, we are like the Gentiles, living in darkness and the shadow of death, yet once again the gospel is proclaimed to us, as it was the first time in Palestine a long time ago.

PATRISTIC TEXTS ON
THE GOSPEL OF LUKE

AUGUSTINE OF HIPPO (DIED 430). Augustine is one of the most prolific of the Church Fathers. His collected works including his theological orations, sermons, letters, and pastoral reflections take up several bookshelves in a library. He is remembered not only as a bishop and administrator of the Church but a true pastor, caring for his flock in Hippo and preaching the gospel of the Lord. There are numerous biographies about his life as well as his famous autobiography called *The Confessions* where he speaks about the spiritual life in general and his own personal journey to Christianity as well.

Augustine was born in north Africa to Patricius and Monica. His father Patricius was a local government official who was a pagan and Monica was a devout Christian who prayed for her son Augustine's conversion to the Christian faith. His father sent him to the north African city of Carthage where he studied law and rhetoric. He eventually fell into the heretical teachings of Manichesim which was taught by Mani. Manichesim was based on a gnostic teaching of duality that the flesh was bad and the spirit is good. Manicheism was very popular during this time and many priests and bishops had to fight against these false teachings. Eventually Augustine traveled to Rome where he met Ambrose, Bishop of Milan. Through many conversations with Ambrose, Augustine realized his errors and accepted to be baptized into the Christian faith. He was baptized sometime in great Lent in 387.

In 396, Augustine became the bishop of Hippo, a small city in North Africa where he served until his death in 438. Augustine lived an austere lifestyle choosing to live in a monastic community rather in a special bishop's residence. The monastic community revolved around regular hours of prayer, community work, and time for reading and contemplation. Eventually Augustine wrote down their way of life in the Monastic Rules which are still used today by the Augustinian Brothers who follow the Rule of St. Augustine in the Catholic Church.

As was stated previously, Augustine was a prolific orator and theologian. He delivered many sermons and theological orations in his cathedral. Like Leo, Augustine had a pastoral heart and his sermons reflect his devotion to the scriptures. Unfortunately many scholars have focused their attention more on his theological writings which are many, yet his commentaries on the scriptures are worth more research and study. His homilies on Matthew and on the other gospels show a connection between the gospels and daily life, looking to Jesus Christ as the supreme example of love.

FOR FURTHER READING:

Augustine of Hippo, *Confessions*, Garry Wills (ed.) (NY: Penguin, 2006).

_____, *The Monastic Rules* (NY: New City Press, 2004).

Brown, Peter, *Augustine of Hippo*, Rev. Ed. (Berkeley, The University of California Press, 2000).

O'Donnell, James J., *Augustine: A New Biography* (New York, Harper Perennial, 2005).

Wills, Garry, *Saint Augustine* (New York, Penguin, 1999).

ON THE WORDS OF THE GOSPEL, LUKE XIV. 16,
"A CERTAIN MAN MADE A GREAT SUPPER"

1. Holy lessons have been set forth before us, to which we should both give ear, and upon which by the Lord's help I would deliver some observations. In the Apostolic lesson thanks are rendered unto the Lord for the faith of the Gentiles, of course, because it was His work. In the Psalm we have said, "O God of hosts, turn us, and show us Thy Face, and we shall be saved." In the Gospel we have been called to a supper; yea, rather others have been called, we not called, but led; not only led, but even forced. For so have we heard, that "a certain Man made a great supper." Who is this Man, but "the Mediator between God and men, the Man Christ Jesus"? He sent that those who had been invited might come, for the hour was now come, that they should come. Who are they who had been invited, but those who had been called by the Prophets who were sent before? When? Of old, ever since the Prophets were sent, they invited to Christ's supper. They were sent then to the people of Israel. Often were they sent, often did they call men, to come at the hour of supper. But they received those who invited them, refused the supper. What means "they received those who invited them, refused the supper"? They read the Prophets and killed Christ. But when they killed Him, then though they knew it not, they prepared a Supper for us. When the Supper was now prepared, when Christ had been offered up, when the Supper of the Lord, which the faithful know, had been set forth after the resurrection of Christ, and established by His Hands and Mouth, were the Apostles sent to them, to whom the Prophets had been sent before. "Come ye to the supper."

2. They who would not come made excuses. And how did they excuse themselves? There were three excuses: "One said, I have bought a farm, and I go to see it; have me excused. Another said, I have bought five pairs of oxen, and I go to prove them; I pray thee have me excused. A third said, I have married a wife, have me excused; I cannot come."

Do we suppose that these are not the excuses, which hinder all men, who decline to come to this supper? Let us look into them, discuss, find them out; but only that we may beware. In the purchase of the farm, the spirit of domination is marked out; therefore pride is rebuked. For men are delighted to have a farm, to hold, to possess it, to have men in it under them, to have dominion. An evil vice, the first vice. For the first man wished to have dominion, in that he would not that any should have dominion over him. What is to have dominion, but to take pleasure in one's own power? There is a greater power, let us submit ourselves to it, that we may be able to be safe. "I have bought a farm, have me excused." Having discovered pride, he would not come.

3. "Another said, I have bought five pairs of oxen." Would it not have been enough, have bought oxen"? Something beyond doubt there is, which by its very obscurity challenges us to seek out, and understand; and in that it is shut, He exhorteth us to knock. The five pairs of oxen are the senses of this body. There are numbered five senses of this body, as is known to all; and they who, it may be, do not consider it, will doubtless perceive it on being reminded of it. There are then found to be five senses of this body. In the eyes is the sight, the hearing in the ears, the smell in the nose, the taste in the mouth, the touch in all the members. We have perception of white and black, and things colored in whatever way, light and dark, by the sight. Harsh and musical sounds, we have perception of by the hearing. Of sweet and offensive smells, we have perception by the smell. Of things sweet and bitter by the taste. Of things hard and soft, smooth and rough, warm and cold, heavy and light, by the touch. They are five, and they are pairs. Now that they are pairs, is seen most easily in the case of the three first senses. There are two eyes, two ears, two nostrils; see three pairs. In the mouth, that is in the sense of taste, a certain doubling is found, because nothing affects the taste, unless it is, touched by the tongue and the palate. The pleasure of the flesh which pertains to the touch, has this doubling in a less obvious way.

For there is both an outer and an inner touch. And so it too is double. Why are they called pairs of oxen? Because by these senses of the body, earthly things are sought for. For oxen turn up the earth. So there are men far off from faith, given up to earthly things, occupied in the things of the flesh; who will not believe anything but what they attain to by the five senses of their body. In those five senses do they lay down for themselves the rules of their whole will. "I will not believe," says one, "anything but what I see.

See, here is what I know, and am sure of Such a thing is white, or black, or round, or square, or colored so and so; this I know, am sensible of, have a hold of; nature itself teaches it me. I am not forced to believe what you cannot show me. Or it is a voice: I perceive that it is a voice; it sings well, it sings ill, it is sweet, it is harsh. I know, I know this, it has come to me. There is a good or a bad smell: I know, I perceive it. This is sweet, this is bitter; this is salt, this insipid. I know not what you would tell me more. By the touch I know what is hard, what is soft; what is smooth, what is rough; what is warm, and what cold. What more would you show me?"

4. By such an impediment was our Apostle Thomas held back, who as to the Lord Christ, the resurrection that is of Christ, would not believe even his own eyes only. "Unless," says he, "I put my fingers into the places of the nails and wounds, and unless I put my hand into His side, I will not believe." And the Lord who could have risen again without any vestige of a wound, kept the scars, that they might be touched by the doubting Apostle, and the wounds of his heart be healed. And yet as designing to call to His supper others, against the excuse of "the five pairs of oxen," He said, "Blessed they who do not see, and believe." We, my Brethren, who have been called to this supper, have not been kept back by "these five pairs." For we have not in this age desired to see the Face of the Lord's Body, nor have we longed to hear the Voice proceeding oat of the mouth of that Body; we have not sought in Him for any passing odor. A certain "woman anointed Him with most costly ointment," that "house was filled with the odor;" but we were not there; lo, we did not smell, yet we believe. He gave to the disciples the Supper consecrated by His Own Hands; but we did not sit clown at that Feast, and yet we daily eat this

same Supper by faith. And do not think it strange that in that supper which He gave with His Own Hand, one was present without faith: the faith that appeared, afterwards was more than a compensation for that faithlessness then. Paul was not there who believed, Judas was there who betrayed. How many now too in this same Supper, though they saw not then that table, nor beheld with their eyes, nor tasted with their mouths, the bread which the Lord took in His Hands, yet because it is the same as is now prepared, how many now also in this same Supper, "eat and drink judgment to themselves"?

5. But whence arose an occasion, so to say, to the Lord, to speak of this supper? One of them that sat at meat with Him (for He was at a feast, whither He had been invited), had said, "Blessed are they who eat bread in the kingdom of God." He sighed as though after distant things, and the Bread Himself was sitting down before him. Who is the Bread of the kingdom of God, but He who saith, "I am the Living Bread which came down from heaven "? Do not get thy mouth ready, but thine heart. On this occasion it was that the parable of this supper was set forth. Lo, we believe in Christ, we receive Him with faith. In receiving Him we know what to think of. We receive but little, and we are nourished in heart. It is not then what is seen, but what is believed, that feeds us. Therefore we too have not sought for that outward sense; nor have we said, "Let them believe who have seen with their eyes, and handled with their hands the Lord Himself after His resurrection, if what is said be true; we do not touch Him, why should we believe?" If we were to entertain such thoughts, we should be kept back from the supper by those "five pairs of oxen." That ye may know, Brethren, that not the gratification of these five senses, which softens and ministers pleasure, but a kind of curiosity was denoted, He did not say, "'I have bought five pairs of oxen,' and I go to feed them;" but, "I go to prove them." He who wishes to "prove "by "the pairs of oxen," does not wish to be in doubt, just as St. Thomas by these "pairs" did not wish to be in doubt. "Let me see, let me touch, let me put in my fingers." "'Behold,' saith the Lord, 'put in thy fingers along My Side, and be not unbelieving.' For thy sake have

I been slain; at the place which thou wishest to touch, have I shed My Blood, that I might redeem thee; and dost thou still doubt of Me, unless thou touch Me? Behold, this too I grant; behold, this too I show thee; touch, and believe; find out the place of My wound, heal the wound of thy doubting."

6. "The third said, I have married a wife." This is the pleasure of the flesh, which is a hindrance to many: and I would that it were so only without, and not within! There are men who say, "There is no happiness for a man, if he have not the pleasures of the flesh." These are they whom the Apostle censures, saying, "'Let us eat and drink, for to-morrow we shall die.' Who hath risen to this life from the other? Who hath ever told us what goes on there? We take away with us, what in the time present makes our happiness." He that speaks thus, "has married a wife," attaches himself to the flesh, places his delight in the pleasures of flesh, excuses himself from the supper; let him look well to it that he die not by an inward famine. Attend to John, the holy Apostle and Evangelist; "Love not the world, neither the things that are in the world." O ye who come to the Supper of the Lord, "Love not the world, neither the things that are in the world." He did not say, "Have not;" but, "Love not." Thou hast had, possessed, loved. The love of earthly things, is the bird-lime of the spirit's wings. Lo, thou hast desired, thou hast stuck fast. "Who will give thee wings as of a dove?" When wilt thou fly, whither thou mayest in deed, seeing thou hast perversely wished to rest here, where thou hast to thy hurt stuck fast? "Love not the world," is the divine trumpet. By the voice of this trumpet unceasingly is it proclaimed to the compass of the earth, and to the whole world, "Love not the world, neither the things that are in the world.

Whosoever loveth the world, the love of the Father is not in him. For all that is in the world, is the lust of the flesh, and the lust of the eyes, and the ambition of life." He begins at the last with which the Gospel ends. He begins at that, at which the Gospel made an end. "The lust of the flesh, I have married a wife. The lust of the eyes, I have bought five pairs of oxen. The ambition of life, I have bought a farm."

7. Now these senses are denoted by the mention of the eyes only, the whole by a part, because the pre-eminence in the five senses belongs to the eyes. Wherefore though sight belongs peculiarly to the eyes, we are accustomed to use the word "seeing" through all the five senses. How? In the first place, in relation to the eyes themselves we say; "See how white it is, look and see how white it is:" this has relation to the eyes. Hear and see how musical it is! Could we say conversely, "Hear and see how white it is"? This expression, "see," runs through all the senses; whereas the distinguishing expression of the other senses does not in its turn run through it. "Mark and see how musical; smell and see how agreeable it is; taste and see how sweet it is; touch and see how soft it is." And yet surely since they are senses, we should rather say thus; "Hear and be sensible how musical it is; smell and be sensible how agreeable it is; taste and be sensible how sweet it is; touch and be sensible how hot it is; handle and be sensible how smooth it is; handle and be sensible how soft it is." But we say none of these. For thus the Lord Himself after His resurrection when He appeared to His disciples, and when though they saw Him they still wavered in faith supposing that they saw a spirit, said, "Why do ye doubt, and why do thoughts arise in your hearts? See My Hands and My Feet." It is not enough to say, "See;" He saith, "Touch, and handle, and see." "Look and see, handle and see; with the eyes alone see, and see by all the senses." Because He was looking for the inner sense of faith, He offered Himself to the outward senses of the body. We have made no attainment in the Lord by these outward senses, we have heard with our ears, have believed with our heart; and this hearing not from His mouth, but from the mouth of His preachers, from their mouths who were already at the supper, and who by the pouring forth of what they there drunk in invited us.

8. Let us away then with vain and evil excuses, and come we to the supper by which we may be made fat within. Let not the puffing up of pride keep us back, let it not lift us up, nor unlawful curiosity scare us, and turn us away from God; let not the pleasure of the flesh hinder us from the pleasure of the heart. Let us come, and be filled.

And who came but the beggars, the "maimed," the "halt," the "blind"? But there came not thither the rich, and the whole, who walked, as they thought, well, and saw acutely; who had great confidence in themselves, and were therefore in the more desperate case, in proportion as they were more proud. Let the beggars come, for He inviteth them, "who, though He was rich, for our sakes became poor, that we beggars through His poverty might be enriched." Let the maimed come, "for they that are whole need not a physician, but they that are in evil case." Let the halt come who may say to Him, "Set in order my steps in Thy paths." Let the blind come who may say, "Enlighten mine eyes, that I may never sleep in death." Such as these came at the hour, when those who had been first invited, had been rejected for their own excuses: they came at the hour, they entered in from the streets and lanes of the city. And the servant "who had been sent," brought answer, "Lord, it is done as Thou hast commanded, and yet there is room." "Go out," saith He," into the highways and hedges, and compel those whom thou shall find to come in." Whom thou shall find wait not till they choose to come, compel them to come in. I have prepared a great supper, a great house, I cannot suffer any place to be vacant in it. The Gentiles came from the streets and lanes: let the heretics come from the hedges, here they shall find peace. For those who make hedges, their object is to make divisions. Let them be drawn away from the hedges, let them be plucked up from among the thorns. They have stuck fast in the hedges, they are unwilling to be compelled. Let us come in, they says of our own good will. This is not the Lord's order, "Compel them," saith he, "to come in." Let compulsion be found outside, the will arise within.

CYRIL OF ALEXANDRIA (DIED 386). Cyril of Alexandria was one of the most prolific of the Church Fathers, writing commentaries on scripture, marriage, as well as other theological topics for catechesis and instruction in the faith. He also lived and wrote during the Christological debates with the famous Nestorius. This was a very difficult period in the Church, a time when there were many debates, discussions, and agreements regarding Jesus human and divine nature. Because of his theological background and expertise he attended the Council of Constantinople in 381 where the Fathers affirmed the full Nicene Faith and when the Nicene-Constantinopolitan Creed was affirmed and accepted.

Cyril wrote two major commentaries on scripture, one on the gospel of John and the other on the gospel of Luke. A short excerpt from one of his sermons on Luke is included for your edification and instruction. As was stated in the introduction to this book, the reader is encouraged to read and reflect on the writings of the early Church Fathers as a way to see how they read and interpreted the scriptures. Their writings offer us insight and information as to the many pearls of wisdom in the Bible.

FOR FURTHER READING:

John McGuckin, *St. Cyril of Alexandria and the Christological Controversy* (Crestwood, NY: St. Vladimir's Seminary Press, 2004).

George Dragas, *St. Cyril of Alexandria's Teaching on the Priesthood* (Rollinsford, NH: Orthodox Research Institute, 2003).

Norman Russell *Cyril of Alexandria* (NY: Rutledge Press, 2000)

SERMON XI. The Eleventh Sermon of the Commentary upon the Gospel of Luke by the Holy Cyril, Archbishop of Alexandria, upon the Manifestation of Our Lord.

And it came to pass, that when all the people were baptized, Jesus also was baptized: and as He was praying, the heavens were opened, and the Holy Ghost descended upon Him in bodily form like a dove. And there was a voice from heaven, saying, Thou art my beloved Son; in Thee I am well pleased. And Jesus Himself was beginning to be about thirty years old.

Again come, that fixing our mind intently upon the Evangelic Scriptures, we may behold the beauty of the truth. Come let us direct the penetrating and accurate eyes of the mind unto the mystery of Christ; let us view with wonder the admirable skill of the divine economy: for so shall we see His glory. And thus to act is for our life: as He Himself assures us, when speaking unto God the Father in heaven, "Those things are life eternal: to know Thee Who alone art true; and Jesus Christ, Whom Thou hast sent." How therefore was He sent? and what was the manner of His coming unto us? For being by nature God That filleth all, how, as the blessed John the Evangelist said, "was He in the world," Himself being Lord? And how was He sent by the Father, when as God He is the Creator and Sustainer of all things? For all things were established by Him.

The wise John the Evangelist then teaches us, saying, "And the Word was made flesh." But perchance some one will say, 'What then? Having ceased to be the Word, did He change into being flesh? Did He fall from His Majesty, having undergone a transformation unto something which previously He was not?' Not so, we say. Far from it. For by nature He is unchangeable and immutable. In saying, therefore, that the Word became flesh, the Evangelist means a man like unto us. For we also are often called flesh ourselves. For it is written, "And all flesh shall see the salvation of God," meaning thereby that every man shall see it. While therefore He immutably retains that "which He was, yet as having under this condition assumed our likeness, He is said to have been made flesh.

Behold Him, therefore, as a man, enduring with us the things that belong to man's estate, and fulfilling all righteousness, for the plan of salvation's sake. And this thou learnest from what the Evangelist says: "And it came to pass that when all the people were baptized, Jesus also was baptized, and prayed." Was He too then in need of holy baptism? But what benefit could accrue to Him from it? The Only-begotten Word of God is Holy of the Holy: so the Seraphim name Him in their praises: so everywhere the law names Him: and the company of the holy prophets accords with the writings of Moses. What is it that we gain by holy baptism? Plainly the remission of our sins. But in Jesus there was nought of this; "for He did no sin: neither was guile found "in His mouth," as the Scripture saith, "He was holy, harmless, undefiled, separate from sins, and made higher than the heavens," according to the words of the divine Paul.

But yes! perchance some one will say, who has been ill instructed in the faith, 'Was it then God the Word that was baptized? Was He in need of being made partaker of the Holy Ghost? Not at all. Therefore it is that we affirm, that the man who was of the seed of David, and united unto Him by conjunction was baptized and received the Spirit.' The Indivisible therefore is divided by you into two souls: and because He was baptized when, thirty years old, He was made holy, as you say, by being baptized. Was He therefore not holy until He arrived at His thirtieth year? Who will assent to you, when thus you corrupt the right and blameless faith? For "there is one Lord Jesus Christ," as it is written. But this we affirm: that He was not separate from Him, and by Himself when baptized and made partaker of the Holy Ghost: for we know, both that He is God, and without stain, and Holy of the Holy: for we confess that "of His fullness have all we received." For the Holy Spirit indeed proceedeth from God the Father, but belongeth also to the Son. It is even often called the Spirit of Christ, though proceeding from God the Father. And to this Paul will testify, saying, at one time, "They that are in the flesh cannot please God: but ye are not in the flesh, but in the spirit, if so be the Spirit of God dwelleth in you. But if any one have not the Spirit of Christ, he is none of His." And again, "But because ye are sons, God hath sent the Spirit of His Son into your hearts, crying, Father, our Father." The Holy Spirit therefore proceedeth indeed as I said from God the Father, but His Only-begotten Word, as being both by nature and verily Son, and resplendent with the Father's dignities, ministereth It to the creation, and bestoweth It on those that are worthy. Yea verily He said, "All things that the Father hath are mine."

But let us retort upon those who pervert the right belief this question; 'How can He Who received the Spirit, if He be, according to your phrase, a man, and the Son separately and by Himself, baptize with the Holy Ghost, and Himself give the Holy Spirit to them who are baptized?' For to be able to impart the Spirit to men suiteth not any one whatsoever of things created, but, together with God's other attributes, is the distinct property of Almighty God alone. But He Who gave It was man: for the wise John said, "After me cometh a Man, Who was before me … He shall baptize you with the Holy Ghost and with fire." As therefore it is unbefitting God the Word, regarded as God the Word, to draw near unto holy baptism, and be made partaker of the Spirit, so in like manner it is altogether incredible, or rather impossible to believe that the ability to baptize men with the Holy Ghost, is the act of a mere man with nothing in Him superior to ourselves.

How then will the mystery be true? In that for our aid He assumed a kind of adaptation. The divine Word became man, even "He Who was in the form of God the Father, and thought it not robbery to be equal unto God," as most wise Paul says, "but took the form of a slave, being made in the likeness of men, and humbling Himself to poverty." Enquire therefore Who He was that was first in the likeness of God the Father, and could be regarded as on an equality with Him, but took the form of a slave, and became then a man, and besides this made Himself poor. Was it He of the seed of David, as they argue, Whom they specially regard separately and by Himself as the other Son, distinct from the Word of God the Father? If so, let them shew that He ever was on an equality with the Father. Let them shew how He assumed the form of a slave. Or what shall we say was that form of a slave? And how did He empty Himself? For what is poorer than human nature? He therefore Who is the exact image of God the Father, the likeness, and visible expression of His person, Who shines resplendent in equality unto Him, Who by right of nature is free, and the yoke of Whoso kingdom is put upon all creation, — He it is Who took the form of a slave, that is, became a man, and made Himself poor by consenting to endure these human things, sin only excepted.

But how then, they object, was He baptized, and received also the Spirit? To which we reply, that He had no need of holy baptism, being wholly pure and spotless, and holy of the holy. Nor had He need of the Holy Ghost: for the Spirit That proceedeth from God the Father is of Him, and equal to Him in substance. We must now therefore at length hear what is the explanation of the economy. God in his love to man provided for us a way of salvation and of life. For believing in the Father, Son, and Holy Ghost, and making this confession before many witnesses, we wash away all the filth of sin, and are enriched by the communication of the Holy Spirit, and made partakers of the divine nature, and gain the grace of adoption. It was necessary therefore that the Word of the Father, when He humbled Himself unto emptiness, and deigned to assume our likeness, should become for our sakes the pattern and way of every good work. For it follows, that He Who in every thing is first, must in this also set the example. In order therefore that we may learn both the power itself of holy baptism, and how much we gain by approaching so great a grace, He commences the work Himself; and, having been baptized, prays that you, my beloved, may learn that never-ceasing prayer is a thing most fitting for those who have once been counted worthy of holy baptism.

And the Evangelist says that the heavens were opened, as having long been closed. For Christ said, "Forthwith shall ye see the heavens opened, and the angels of God ascending and descending upon the Son of man." For both the flock above and that below being now made one, and one chief Shepherd appointed for all, the heavens were opened, and man upon earth brought near to the holy angels.

And the Spirit also again came down as at a second commencement of our race: and upon Christ first, Who received it not so much for His own sake as for ours: for by Him and in Him are we enriched with all things. Most suitably therefore to the economy of grace does He endure with us the things of man's estate: for where otherwise shall we see Him emptied, Whose in His divine nature is the fullness? How became He poor as we are, if He were not conformed to our poverty? How did He empty Himself, if He refused to endure the measure of human littleness?

Having taken therefore Christ as our pattern, let us draw near to the grace of holy baptism, that so we may gain boldness to pray constantly, and lift up holy hands to God the Father, that He may open the heavens also unto us, and send down upon us too the Holy Ghost, to receive us as sons. For He spake unto Christ at the time of holy baptism, as though having by Him and in Him accepted man upon earth to the sonship, "This is My beloved Son, in Whom I am well pleased." For He Who is the Son by nature and in truth, and the Only-begotten, when He became like unto us, is specially declared to be the Son of God, not as receiving this for Himself: — for He was and is, as I said, very Son: — but that He might ratify the glory unto us. For He has been made our firstfruits, and firstborn, and second Adam: for which reason it is said, that "in Him all things have become new:" for having put off the oldness that was in Adam, we have gained the newness that is in Christ: by Whom and with Whom, to God the Father, be glory and dominion with the Holy Ghost, for ever and ever, Amen.

JOHN CHRYSOSYOM (DIED 407). John was born in Antioch in 347. Like Gregory, John had a classical education that included both rhetoric and philosophy. John studied under the direction of the great philosopher Libanius. When John returned to Antioch he befriended Bishop Meletius who baptized John and then ordained him to the diaconate. After baptism, Chrysostom entered the dessert for six years. He put himself under the care and guidance of Diodore of Tarsus, the famous Antiochene exegete. Diodore established a school for the learning and interpretation of scripture and was sought out as one of the greatest teachers of scripture in the Christian East. His students lived an austere lifestyle devoted to fasting and prayer with the remainder of time devoted to studying Scripture.

Under the new bishop Flavian, John assisted in assisting the poor and needy, and even though he was a deacon, preached frequently in Church. In 398 John was appointed bishop in Constantinople where he found himself at the center of the Roman Empire. While in Constantinople John had different duties then when he was a priest yet he still continued to preach and teach as was his custom. As bishop, John's responsibilities were devoted the financial well being of the diocese as well as maintaining peace and concord among the clergy and local parish churches. John was the chief pastor in the capital city and therefore had much greater responsibilities then when he was a priest. However, while his obligations took him to various places and locations John always cared for his community and preached sermons about repentance, love, forgiveness, and salvation.

Throughout his ecclesiastical career at Antioch and Constantinople John devoted himself to preaching the gospel and ministering to the church of Christ. Chrysostom encountered a lot of resistance to the truth from the rich upper class of society and the political leaders. However, John's only weapon was gospel of Christ and he used it whenever he had the opportunity. The vast number of his sermons and homilies that survive testify to this fact. John certainly earned the name "golden mouth" and priests and pastors still look to him as an example of as a true pastor of Christ's flock. St. John is com-

memorated on November 13 and on January 30 together with, Basil
the Great and Gregory the Theologian.

FOR FURTHER READING:

St. John Chrysostom, *On Marriage and Family*, translated by Catherine P. Roth and David Anderson (Crestwood, NY: St. Vladimir's
Seminary Press, 1986).

_____, *On Wealth and Poverty*, translated by Catherine P. Roth
(Crestwood, NY: St. Vladimir's Seminary Press, 1984).

_____, *Six Books on the Priesthood*, translated by Graham Neville
(Crestwood, NY: St. Vladimir's Seminary Press, 1984).

_____, *Baptismal Instructions*, translated Paul W. Harkins (Mah-
wah, NJ: Paulist Press, 1963).

_____, *On The Cult of the Saints*, translated Wendy Mayer with Bro-
wen Neil (Crestwood, NY: St. Vladimir's Seminary Press, 2006).

Wendy Mayer and Pauline Allen, *John Chrysostom* (NY: Routledge,
2000).

J. N. D Kelly, *Golden Mouth: The Story of John Chrysostom: Asectic,
Preacher, Bishop* (Grand Rapids, MI: Baker Books, 1995).

DISCOURSE I.

A Homily Delivered at Antioch
On the Second Day of the Month

Yesterday, we alleged against such feasters the testimony of St
Paul, who says, "Whether ye eat or drink, or whatsoever ye do, do
all to the glory of God," (1 Cor. x. 31.) Today, we shall show them the
Lord of Paul not only advising or counseling to abstain from luxury,
but also punishing and inflicting penalties on one who lived in luxury; for the narrative of the rich man and Lazarus, and of the things
which befell them, proves nothing less than this. And rather than that
our consideration of this subject should be superficial, I will read to
you the parable from the commencement. "There was a certain rich
man, which was clothed in purple and fine linen, and fared sumptuously every day. And there was a certain beggar named Lazarus,
which was laid at his gate, full of sores, and desiring to be fed with the
crumbs which fell from the rich man's table: moreover, the dogs came
and licked his sores" (Luke xvi. 19–21).

Now for what reason did the Lord speak to them in parables? Why
also did He explain some of these, and leave others unexplained? And
what indeed is a parable? These, and other questions of this nature,
we will reserve until another opportunity, so as not to digress from
the argument now claiming our attention.

One thing, however, we will ask: Which of the evangelists has
delivered to us this parable as spoken by Christ? Which then is it?
It is St Luke only. For it is also necessary to know that, of the things
which are related, some are related by all four; some, as by special
information, by one only. And why? In order that the reading of the
other Gospels might be necessary, and that their agreement with each
other might be made manifest. For if they all delivered all the events,
we should not examine them all with such care, since one only would
be sufficient to inform us about everything. If, again, all spoke of different events, we should fail to discover their agreement. On this ac-

count they all wrote many things in common, while at the same time each received and delivered matters peculiar to himself.

To return, however, to Christ's teaching in the parable. It is this: A certain man, it is said, living in great wickedness, was rich; and he experienced no ill fortune, but all good things flowed to him as from a perennial fountain. For that nothing undesirable happened to him — no cause of trouble — none of the ills of human life — is implied when it is said, that "he fared sumptuously every day." And that he lived wickedly is clear from the end allotted to him, and even before his end, from the neglect which he displayed in the case of the poor man; for that he felt pity neither for the poor man at his gate nor for any other, he himself showed. For if he had no pity on the man continually laid at his gate, and placed before his eyes, whom every day, once or twice, or oftentimes, as he went in and out, he was obliged to see; — for the man was not placed in a by-way, nor in a hidden and narrow place, but in a spot where the rich man, in his continual coming-in and going-out, was obliged, even if unwilling, to look upon him; — if, therefore, the rich man did not pity him lying there in such suffering, and living in such distress, — yea, rather, all his life long in misery because of sickness, and that of the most grievous kind, — would he ever have been moved with compassion towards any of the afflicted whom he might casually meet? For though on one occasion the rich man passed him by, it was likely that he would manifest some feeling the next day; and if even then he disregarded the poor man, still on the third day, or the fourth, or even after that, he might be expected in some way to be moved to compassion, even if he were more cruel than the wild beasts. But he had no feeling: he was more severe and harsh than that judge who neither feared God nor regarded man. For the judge, though so cruel and stern, was moved by the perseverance of the widow to be gracious and listen to her petition; but this man could not even thus be induced to give aid to the poor man, notwithstanding that his petition was not like that of the widow, but much easier and fairer. For she requested aid against her enemies, while this poor man was entreating that his hunger might be allayed, and that he should not be allowed to perish. The widow also caused trouble by her entreaties; but this man, though often in the day seen by the rich man, only lay without speaking: and this circumstance was quite sufficient to soften a heart harder than stone. When we are urged, we frequently feel annoyed; but when we see those who need our help remaining in perfect silence and saying not a word, and though always failing to gain their object, not bearing it hardly, but. only appearing before us in silence, even though we are more unfeeling than the very stones, we are shamed and moved by such exceeding humility. There is also another circumstance of not less weight, namely, that the very appearance of the poor man was pitiable, since he was emaciated by hunger and long sickness. Yet none of these things influenced that cruel man.

First, then, there was this vice of cruelty and inhumanity in a degree that could not be exceeded. For it is not the same thing for one living in poverty not to assist those who are in need, as for one who enjoys such luxury to neglect others who are wasting away through hunger. Again, it is not the same thing for one to pass by a poor man when he sees him once or twice, as to see him every day without being moved by the oft-recurring sight to pity and benevolence. Again, it is not the same thing for one who is in difficulties and anxiety, and troubled in soul, not to help his neighbor, as for one enjoying such good fortune and unbroken prosperity, to neglect others who are perishing from hunger, and to shut up his bowels of compassion, and not rather, for the very sake of his own happiness, to become more benevolent. For know this of a truth, that unless we are the most cruel of all men, we are, by our very nature, apt, by our own prosperity, to be rendered milder and more gentle. But this rich man did not grow better on account of his prosperity, but remained ill-natured; or rather had, deep in his disposition, cruelty and inhumanity greater than that of a beast of the field.

Still it came to pass that a man living in wickedness and inhumanity enjoyed every kind of good fortune, and a just and virtuous man lingered in the greatest ills. For that Lazarus was a just man is made plain, as in the other case, by his end, and even before his end, by his patience and poverty. Do you not, indeed, seem to see these things present before our eyes? The ship of the rich man was laden with merchandise, and sailed with a fair wind. But do not marvel; for it was borne on to shipwreck, since he was not willing to bestow its burden wisely. Would you that I should give another proof of his wickedness? It is his living in luxury every day without fear. For this in truth is the height of wickedness; and not only now, when we are required to show such moderation, but even in the beginning, under the old covenant, when there was no revelation of the need of this self-control. For hear what the prophet says: "Woe to them that come to an evil day, that come near, and that make a Sabbath of lies" (Amos vi. 3, LXX).

The Jews suppose that the Sabbath was given to them for the sake of ease. But this is not the object of it; but it was in order that, separating themselves from, worldly affairs, they might bestow all that leisure on spiritual things. For that the Sabbath was not for the sake of idleness, but for spiritual work, is clear from its very circumstances. The priest, on that day, does a double portion of work, a single sacrifice being offered each common day, while on that day he is commanded to offer a double sacrifice. And if the Sabbath were for the sake of idleness, the priest before all others ought to be idle. Since therefore the Jews, separating themselves from worldly things, devoted not themselves to spiritual things, to temperance, and gentleness, and hearing the divine word, but did the very opposite, feasting, drinking, indulging in excess and luxury; on this account it is, that the prophet condemns them. For he says, "Woe to them that come to an evil day," and, in continuation, "that make a Sabbath of lies." He shows by that which follows how their Sabbath became unprofitable. How then did they make it unprofitable? By their working wickedness, living in luxury, drinking, and doing numberless other base and vile acts. And that this charge is true, hear what follows; for he intimates that which I am affirming, by that which he immediately adds, saying: "That lie upon beds of ivory, and stretch themselves upon their couches, and eat the lambs out of the flock, and the calves out of the midst of the stall; that drink refined wine, and anoint themselves with the chief ointments" (Amos vi. 4, 6).

Thou didst receive the Sabbath that thou mightest purify thy soul from wickedness; but thou hast increased wickedness. For what can be worse than this effeminacy — this "sleeping upon beds of ivory?" The other sins, as drinking, covetousness, or prodigality, may be accompanied with some small amount of pleasure; but the sleeping on beds of ivory, what pleasure is there in it? Is more refreshing or sweeter sleep brought to us by the beauty of the couch? Nay, rather this beauty is more burdensome and more troublesome to us, if we reflect upon the matter. For whenever thou dost consider that while thou art sleeping on an ivory couch, another fellow-creature is not even able to enjoy the certainty of having bread to eat, will not conscience condemn thee and rise up to accuse this wrong? And if to sleep on an ivory couch be a reproach, what defense can we make when the bed is also decked with silver? Dost thou wish to know the true beauty of a couch? I will show thee the adornment, not of a couch belonging to one in private life, nor to a soldier, but to a king. Though thou shouldst be of all men the most desirous of honour, be assured that thou couldst not wish to have a couch more becoming than that of this king. It is also not that of an ordinary king, but of a very great king, a king of all kings most kingly, and even to this day magnified in the whole world. I show thee the couch of the blessed David. Of what kind then was it? It was not decked with silver and gold, but everywhere with tears and confessions. And this he himself says, speaking thus: "All the night make I my bed to swim, and water my couch with my tears" (Ps. vi. 6). Thus with tears was it in all parts adorned as if with pearls.

Mark then with me this godly soul. For although by day manifold cares — about the rulers, about the governors, about the tribes, about the different races, about soldiers, about war, about peace, about affairs of state, about household affairs, about things far off, about things near home, distracted and disturbed him, nevertheless, the leisure time which we all give to sleep he spent in confessions and prayers and tears. And this he did not for one night to cease from it the next, not for two or three nights, after intervals of repose; but he was doing this every night; for "every night," said he, "wash I my bed, and water my couch with my tears," (Ps. vi. 6, *Prayer-book version,*) indicating the abundance of his tears and their continuance. For when all were quiet and at rest, he alone held converse with God; and the eye of Him who never sleepeth was turned towards the man who bewailed and lamented and confessed his indwelling sins. Such a couch as this do thou prepare. For silver ornaments both excite the envy of man and enkindle wrath from above. But such tears as those of David can even extinguish the fire of Gehenna.

Do you wish me to show thee another couch? I mean that of Jacob. He lay on the ground, and a stone was under his head. Therefore also, he saw the symbolical stone, and that ladder on which angels were ascending and descending. Couches of this kind let us also have, that we may see such visions. If we lie upon silver, we not only gain no pleasure, but also endure trouble. For whenever thou dost consider that in the severest cold in the middle of the night, while thou art sleeping on thy couch, the poor man lying on chaff in the porticoes of the baths, covered with straw, is trembling, numb with cold, and fainting with hunger, even if thou shouldst be most stony-hearted, be assured that thou wilt condemn thyself for being content that while thou art luxuriating in things superfluous, *he* is not able to enjoy even the necessaries of life. "No man that warreth," saith the apostle, "entangleth himself with the affairs of this life" (2 Tim. ii. 4). Thou art a spiritual soldier; but such a soldier does not sleep on an ivory bed, but on the ground; he does not use scented unguents, for this is the habit of sensual and dissolute men — of those who live on the stage, or in indolence; and it is not the odor of ointment that thou shouldst have, but that of virtue. The soul is none the more pure when the body is thus scented. Yea, this fragrance of the body and of the dress may even be a sign of inward corruption and uncleanness. For when Satan makes his approaches to corrupt the soul and fill it with all indolence, then also by means of ointments he impresses upon the body the stains which mark its inner defilement. And just as those who suffer continually from flux and catarrh defile their garments and person, constantly discharging these humours; in the same way the soul denies the body with the evil of this corrupt discharge. What noble or useful deed can be expected from a man scented with myrrh and living effeminately, or rather keeping company with meretricious women, and giving himself up to the company of low actors? Rather let the soul exhale spiritual odors, in order that thou mayest in the greatest degree benefit both thyself and thy associates.

For nothing — nothing is worse than luxury. Hear what Moses again says concerning it: "He is waxen fat, he is grown thick, he is increased, he that is beloved kicked," (Deut. xxxii. 15, LXX). And he does not say: "he rebelled," but he "kicked," indicating to us his wildness and intractableness. And again, in another place; "When thou hast eaten and art full, beware that thou forget not the Lord thy God" (Deut. viii. 10, 11). Thus does luxury lead to forgetfulness. Then do thou also, beloved, when thou sittest at table, remember that after the meal thou shouldst pray: and so moderately refresh thyself that thou mayest not through fullness be unable to bend the knee and call upon God. Do you not see beasts of burden, how after feeding, they recommence the journey, they bear loads, they fulfil all the service that falls to their lot? But thou when thou risest from table, art unfit for any work; thou art become useless. How wilt thou avoid being thought less worthy of honour than the very beasts? Wherefore? Because it is then the proper time to be sober and to watch. For the time after meals is the time for thanksgiving; and he who gives thanks should not indulge in excess, but be sober and vigilant. Let us not turn from the table to the couch, but to prayer, that we become not more irrational than the beasts.

I am aware that many will condemn that which is said, as leading to a new and strange manner of living. But I the more condemn the evil customs that are now prevalent amongst us. For that when we rise from food, and from the table, we ought to proceed, not to sleep and the couch, but to prayers and the reading of the Holy Scriptures; this is made most clear by Christ. For when He had feasted the innumerable multitude in the wilderness, He did not dismiss them to lie down to sleep, but called them to hear the divine word.[3] He did not fill them to repletion, nor allow them to fall into excess; but having satisfied their need, he led them to a spiritual feast. Thus let us also act, and let us accustom ourselves to eat so much only as will sustain our higher life, and not hinder and oppress it. For it was not for this that we were born, and exist — namely, that we should eat and drink; but let us eat for this — namely, that we may live. It was not given us at first to live for the sake of eating, but to eat for the sake of living. But we, as if we had come into the world merely to eat, upon this we spend everything.

In order that this charge against luxury may be corroborated, and come home to those who are living in it, let us return in our discourse to Lazarus. And thus the warning will become clearer, and the counsel more effectual, since you will see those who live in excess instructed and corrected, not by words only, but by acts. The rich man lived in this kind of wickedness, and luxuriated day by day, and was splendidly attired; but he was bringing on himself severer punishment, stirring up a fiercer flame, making his condemnation more complete, and the penalty more inexorable.

But the poor man who was cast at his gate grieved not, nor blasphemed, nor complained. He did not say within himself, as many do, "Why is this so? This man living in wickedness and cruelty and inhumanity enjoys all things even beyond his need, and endures no trouble nor any of the unlooked-for reverses that often happen in human affairs. He enjoys unmixed pleasure, while I have not the opportunity of partaking even of necessary food. To this man, who squanders all his substance on parasites and flatterers and wine — to *him* all good things flow like a river; while I live as an object to be gazed at — an object of shame and derision, and am wasting through hunger. Is *this* Providence? Can it be *Justice* that overrules human affairs?"

He did not say any of these things, nor had he them in his mind. How is this manifest? From the circumstance that guardian angels

surrounded him at his death, and bore him away to Abraham's bosom. Had he been a blasphemer, he would not have gained this glory.
Thus also most people wonder at this man merely because of his poverty; but I proceed to show that he endured these ninefold afflictions,
not for punishment, but that he might become more glorious. This
result accordingly happened.

A dreadful thing, in truth, is poverty, as all who have had experience of it know. For no words can express the trouble which they
endure who live in poverty, without knowing the relief of true philosophy. And in the case of Lazarus, there was not only this evil, but
bodily 'weakness superadded, and that in the highest degree. Notice
how it is shown that both these inflictions reached the highest pitch.
That the poverty of Lazarus at that time surpassed all other poverty,
is clear, when it is said that he did not obtain the crumbs which fell
from the rich man's table. And that his weakness had reached the
same pitch as his poverty, beyond which it could not go, this also is
shown when it is said that the dogs licked his sores. He was so feeble
as not to be able to drive away the dogs; but he lay like a living corpse,
seeing their approach, but powerless to keep them at a distance-To
such an extent were his limbs emaciated; so much was he wasted by
bodily sickness; so far was he worn down by trials. You see that poverty and weakness in the highest degree, as it were, besieged his body.
And if each of these evils by itself is unbearable and dreadful, what
adamantine strength must he have who must bear them both united!
Many people are often in ill health, but they do not at the same time
lack necessary food. Others may live in utter poverty, but they may
enjoy health; and the blessing on the one hand may counterbalance
the evil on the other; but in the case we are considering, both these
evils came together.

Suppose, however, that there may be some alleviation even in
weakness and in poverty. But this cannot be, when in such a state
of desertion. For if there were no one connected with him or at his
home, to pity him, yet he might have met with compassion from
some of the beholders, when lying before the public; but in this case

the utter lack of helpers increased the afore-mentioned evils. And the being laid at the gate of the rich man added to his distress. If he had been placed in a desert and uninhabited place when he suffered this neglect, he would not have felt such grief; for the fact of there being no one nigh would have led him, even though unwillingly, to submit to these unavoidable evils; but being placed in the midst of so many people carousing and rejoicing, and meeting with not the slightest attention from any of them, made the thought of his own woes more bitter, and the more inflamed his grief. For we are so constituted as not to be so much distressed by evils when all helpers are at a distance, as when helpers who are near are unwilling to stretch out a hand to aid us. This grief, then, this poor man felt. There was no one either to console him by a word, or to comfort him by a kind act; no friend, no neighbor, no relation, no one of those who saw him; not one of all the corrupt household of the rich man.

Besides, in addition to these things, it would cause another accession of woe to see another man in such prosperity. Not that he was envious and evil-minded, but because it is the nature of us all to feel our own private misfortunes more acutely when we see others in prosperity. And with respect to the rich man, there was another circumstance which would give Lazarus pain. For, in truth, not only by comparing his own ill-fortune with another's prosperity did he feel the more deeply his own woes, but also by the consideration that another who acted with cruelty and inhumanity was in every respect fortunate; while he himself, with his virtue and meekness, suffered extreme misery; and thus, again, he would feel inconsolable grief. For if the rich man had been just, if he had been gentle, if he had been worthy of admiration, full of all virtue, the thought would not thus have grieved Lazarus. But now, when the rich man was living in wickedness, proceeding to the extreme of evil, displaying such inhumanity, and acting as an enemy, passing him by as shamelessly and pitilessly as though he were a stone; and notwithstanding all this was enjoying such prosperity, consider how likely it would be that this state of things would plunge the soul of the poor man in continual

waves of woe! Consider how Lazarus would feel when he saw parasites, flatterers' servants going up and down, coming in and out, as
they hastened about, noisy, drinking, dancing, and displaying every
form of wantonness. For, just as if he had come for the very purpose of being a witness of another's prosperity, he was laid at his gate,
having life only sufficient to make him sensible of his own ills. He
suffered, as it were, shipwreck at the very harbour's mouth, and was
consumed with thirst at the very edge of the spring.

Shall I add to these yet another woe? It is this, — that he could
nowhere see another Lazarus. We ourselves even though we suffer
ten thousand ills, still are able looking at him (Lazarus) to gain effectual comfort and feel great consolation. For to find fellowship
in his private ills, whether they be physical or mental, brings great
alleviation to the sufferer. Lazarus, however, could not look to any
other man suffering the same things as himself; or rather he could
not even hear of any one of those going before him, who had endured
such things. This of itself was enough to becloud his mind. And, besides this, we have to mention another thing: — that he was unable
to console himself with any hope of the resurrection, but thought
that present things are bounded by the present existence, for he lived
under the old dispensation. And if even now, in these days, after such
a revelation of God's character, and the blessed hope of the resurrection, and the knowledge of the punishment laid up for sinners, and
the good things prepared for the righteous, many men are so feeble-
minded and weak as not even to be confirmed by such expectations
as these, what would he, in all probability, endure who was without
such an anchor of hope? This man could not at any time thus console
himself, because the time had not yet arrived when such revelations
were vouchsafed to man. And even in addition to this, there was yet
another thing, namely, that his character was maligned by foolish
men. For the generality of men are accustomed, when they see any
in hunger and thirst, or living in great trouble, not to entertain any
charitable feeling respecting them, but rather to pass judgment on
their life by their misfortunes, and to suppose that they are thus af-

flicted entirely on account of their wickedness; and they say to each other many things of this kind — foolishly no doubt — but still they say so: — "This man, if he were favorably regarded by God, would not have been suffered to be afflicted with poverty and other woes." In this way it happened to Job and to Paul. To the former they said: — "Hath it not often been said to thee in trouble, The force of thy words who can bear? For if thou didst instruct many, and strengthen the weak hands, and raise up the feeble with thy words, and give power to the tottering knees; yet now trouble has come upon thee, and thou art over-anxious. Is not thy fear the offspring of folly" (Job iv. 2–6, LXX). The meaning of these words is this — "If," they say, "thou hadst acted rightly thou wouldst not have suffered these present ills; but thou art paying the penalty of sins and transgressions."

Again concerning Paul, the barbarians spoke in the same strain; when they saw the viper hanging from his hand, they had no favorable opinion of him, but supposed that he was one of those who dare to commit the greatest crimes. This is plain from that which they said: — "This man though he hath escaped the sea, yet vengeance suffereth not to live" (Acts xxviii. 4). This same thing frequently disturbs ourselves not a little. But notwithstanding that the waves of trouble, dashing against each other, were so great, the bark of this poor man was not overwhelmed; and though he was placed as it were in a furnace, he preserved his tranquillity as if refreshed with perpetual dew.

Nor did he say within himself anything of this kind — as it seems many do say, namely: — "This rich man when he departs this life will undergo punishments and penalties, and then *one will have become one again;* but if he there be honoured two will have come to nothing." Now, do not many among yourselves use such expressions in the market, or introduce into the church words which belong to the circus or the theatre? I should be ashamed, and blush to utter such words aloud, were it not necessary to say such things in order that you may avoid the unlicensed mirth and shame and harm springing from the use of such expressions. Many frequently laugh when they say these things; but this is the effect of satanical guile, in order to bring corrupt expressions into common use instead of sound words. Such things as these many constantly repeat in the workshop, in the market, in their houses, — things full of utter unbelief and folly — things that are in reality ridiculous and puerile. For to say, "*if* the wicked when they depart are punished," and not to be fully persuaded in one's own mind that they will in truth be punished, is a mark of unbelief and scepticism. If also it should result, even as it *will* result, even the very *thought* that the evil will enjoy the same rewards as the just, is utter folly.

What dost thou mean, tell me, when thou sayest, if the rich man when he departs should receive punishment, "*one has become one?*" (There is equality.) And how is the saying true? For how many years do you wish that we suppose that he has here enjoyed wealth? Do you wish to suppose *a hundred?* I, for my part, am willing rather to suppose two hundred, or three hundred, or twice as many; or even, if you wish, a thousand, however impossible it may be. *The days of our years,* it is said, *are eighty years,* (alluding to Ps. xc. 10). Suppose, however, a thousand. But can you, I pray, show me in this world a life that has no end? — one that knows no limit, such as is the life of the just in heaven? Tell me then, if some one in the course of a hundred years, seeing for a single night a dream of prosperity; and, after enjoying in his sleep great luxury, should be punished for a hundred years — would you be able to say of him *one has become one,* (there is an equal balance,) and place the one night of dreams as a counterpoise to the hundred years? It is impossible to say so. Think, then, in the same way concerning the life to come. For the proportion that the dream of one night has to the hundred years, the same the present life has to the future life; or, rather, the latter proportion is much the less. As a little drop to the fathomless ocean, so is a thousand years to that future glory and bliss. And what can one say more, except that *that* life has no limit, and knows no end; and that there is as much difference between dreams and realities as there is between our condition in this world and our condition in the next. Besides, even before the future punishment, those who live wickedly are punished now. For do not tell me only of enjoying a sumptuous table, and of being clothed in silken garments, and of being followed by troops of slaves, and of proceeding in state through the public places of resort; but lay open to me the conscience of such a man, and there you shall see within great trouble on account of sins, perpetual dread, tempest, and confusion, and the reason, as in a court of justice, ascending the royal throne of conscience, sitting there as a judge, bringing forward the thoughts as ministers of justice, racking the mind, torturing it on account of sin, and vehemently accusing it; and this state of things is known to no one else, save only God, who sees all that takes place.

Again, he who commits fornication, though he be rich in the highest degree, and though he have no accuser, never ceases inwardly to accuse himself. The pleasure is fleeting, while the pain is lasting; there is fear from all sides and trembling, suspicion, and agony; he fears the by-ways, he trembles at the very shadows, at his own domestics, at those who know his guilt, at those who know it not, at the injured one, at her wronged husband: he goes about bearing with him a keen accuser — his own conscience — being self-condemned, and unable to find the slightest relief. And even on his bed, or at his table, or in the market, or in his house, by day, by night, even in his very dreams he often sees the image of his sin; he lives the life of a Cain, groaning and trembling on the earth; and though no one knows it, he has within himself the unquenchable fire.

This also they who rob and who are covetous suffer; *this* also does the drunkard suffer, and, in short, every one living in sin. It is impossible that *that* tribunal can in any way be influenced. And if we do not follow after virtue, yet we are pained for not following after it; and if we follow vice, as soon as we lose the pleasure that accompanies the sin, we feel the pain. Let us therefore not say concerning those who are prosperous here, and yet do ill, and concerning the just who enjoy felicity in the next world, that "*one becomes one*" (all is equally balanced,) but that "*two come to nothing*" (all the good is on one side.) For, to the just the life here and the life yonder both bring much pleasure; but they who live in wickedness and in luxury are punished both in the life here and the life yonder. For even *here* they are harassed by the expectation of the coming penalty, as well as by the bad opinion in which they are held by all, and by the fact that by the very sin itself their soul is corrupted; and after their departure thither they endure insupportable penalties.

Again, the just, even if they suffer a thousand ills here, are encouraged by pleasant hopes; they have unmixed, sure, and abiding pleasure; and after these things, innumerable blessings accrue to them, as also we see in the case of Lazarus.

Therefore do not say to me that he was full of sores; but mark this — that he had within him a soul more precious than all gold; or rather, mark not only his soul, but also his body; for bodily perfection consists not in stoutness and vigor, but in being able to bear so many and so great afflictions. For, if one have in his body wounds of this kind, he is not therefore to be despised. But rather, if one have in his soul so many defects, for him we should have no regard; — and such was that rich man, covered with wounds within. And as dogs licked the wounds of the one, so the evil spirits aggravated the sins of the other; as the one starved for lack of food, so the other for lack of virtue.

Knowing, therefore, these things, let us act wisely, and let us not say that if God loved such a one, He would not have allowed him to be in poverty. This very thing is the greatest token of love. For "whom the Lord loveth He chasteneth, and scourgeth every son whom He receiveth" (Heb. xii. 6.) And again, "My son, if thou dost purpose to serve the Lord, prepare thy soul for trial, make ready thy heart, and be strong," (Eccl. ii. 1.) Let us then, beloved, cast these vain imaginations away from us, and these common sayings; for "filthiness and foolish talking and jesting, let it not proceed out of your mouth," (Eph. v. 4.) Let us not say such things; and if we see others speaking thus, let us refute them, let us boldly arise and put a stop to such shameless speech. Tell me, if you should see any robber prowling about the road, lying in wait for those that pass by, and plundering the land, secreting gold and silver in caves and hiding-places, and shutting up in such places a great quantity of booty, gaining from this course of life rich garments and many captives; tell me, should you then think him happy on account of such wealth? Or should you think him miserable on account of the judgment about to overtake him? And even if he should escape this, if he should not be delivered into the hand of justice, nor fall into prison, nor have any accuser, nor come to trial, but eat and drink and enjoy great abundance, still we do not think him happy because of present and visible circumstances; but we think him miserable on account of the things which are to come, and to which we look forward.

In the same way reason with yourself concerning the rich and the avaricious. Robbers lie in wait in the way and plunder travellers, and hide the wealth of others in their own lurking-places — in caves or dens. Do not, therefore, think them happy on account of the present, but miserable on account of the future — on account of the fearful judgment, the inevitable account to be rendered — the outer darkness which will envelop them. Even though robbers often escape the hand of men, yet, notwithstanding though we know this, we deprecate for ourselves such a life as theirs, or even for our enemies we should deprecate such an accursed prosperity. Yet with respect to God such a thing cannot be said. No one can escape His judgment, but all who in any way live in covetousness and rapine will undergo the punishment allotted by Him — that deathless punishment which has no end, — in the same way as also did this rich man.

Taking all this, therefore, into consideration, beloved, think those blessed, not who live in wealth, but in virtue; think those miserable, not those who live in poverty, but in wickedness: let us look not at the present, but at the future; let us examine, not the outward appearance, but the conscience of each man; and following after the virtue and the bliss of right actions, let us, whether we be wealthy or poor, emulate Lazarus. He endured not one, nor two, nor three, but many tests of his goodness. These tests were his poverty, his weakness, his lack of helpers, his suffering these evils in a place where there was at hand the means of complete relief, while no one vouchsafed a word of comfort, his seeing him who disregarded him possessing all that

abundance, and not only possessing abundance, but living in wickedness, and suffering no ill; also, his being able to look to no *other Lazarus,* and his being unable to console himself by the thought of the
resurrection. And besides all the aforesaid ills, there was his having
to bear an ill-character among many, for the very reason that he was
a sufferer. There was, not only for two or three days, but for his whole
life, the seeing himself in such circumstances, and the rich man in the
very opposite.

What excuse, therefore, shall we have if, while this man bore all
these excessive evils with such fortitude, we cannot bear even the half
of them? for you are unable — you are unable, I say, to show, or even
to name, any man who has borne such numerous and heavy evils. For
this cause, therefore, Christ brought them before our notice, in order
that whensoever we fall into trouble, seeing in his case the exceeding
greatness of his affliction, we may, from his wisdom and patience, gain
effectual consolation and comfort; for he is set as a general instruc-
tor of the whole world, for all who are suffering any kind of distress;
enabling all to look to one who surpassed them all in the exceeding
greatness of his woes. For all these things, therefore, let us give thanks
unto God — the merciful God; let us reap the benefit of this narrative, continually bearing it in mind, in the assembly, at home, in the
market, yea everywhere; and let us diligently gain all the wealth of
wisdom contained in this parable, in order that we may without grief
pass through evils, and that we may attain the good things in store.
Which benefits may we all be enabled to gain, by the grace and kindness of our Lord Jesus Christ, to whom, with the Father, together with
the Holy Spirit, be praise, honor, adoration, now and ever, even to all
eternity. Amen.

BIBLIOGRAPHY

GENERAL REFERENCES FOR SCRIPTURE STUDY:

Bianchi, Enzo. *Praying the Word: An Introduction to Lectio Divina.* Kalamazoo, MI: Cistercian Publications, 1998.

Johnson, Luke Timothy. *Living Jesus: Learning the Heart of the Gospel.* San Fransisco, CA: Harper Collins, 1999.

Manley, Johanna. *The Bible and the Holy Fathers.* Crestwood, NY: St. Vladimir's Seminary Press.

Mills, William C. *From Pascha to Pentecost: Reflections on the Gospel of John.* Rollinsford, NH: Orthodox Research Institute, 2004.

_____. *Prepare O Bethlehem: Reflections on the Gospel Readings for Nativity and Epiphany.* Rolllinsford, NH: Orthodox Research Institute, 2005.

_____. *Baptize All Nations: Reflections on the Gospel of Matthew During the Pentecost Season.* Rollinsford, NH: Orthodox Research Institute, 2006.

Royster, Archbishop Dmitri. *The Parables.* Crestwood, NY: St. Vladimir's Seminary Press, 1996.

_____. *The Miracles of Christ.* Crestwood, NY: St Vladimir's Seminary Press, 1999.

_____. *The Epistle to the Hebrews.* Crestwood, NY: St. Vladimir's Seminary Press, 2003.

_____. *The Epistle to the Romans.* Crestwood, NY: St. Vladimir's Seminary Press, forthcoming 2007.

Tarazi, Paul N. *The New Testament Introduction: Paul and Mark.* Crestwood, NY: St. Vladimir's Seminary Press, 1999.

INTERNET RESOURCES FOR SCRIPTURE STUDY:

Orthodox Center for the Advancement of Biblical Studies:
   www.ocabs.org

New Testament Gateway:
   www.ntgateway.com

PBS Documentary "From Jesus To Christ":
www.pbs.org/wgbh/page/frontline/religion

SELECT COMMENTARIES ON THE GOSPEL OF LUKE:

Johnson, Luke Timothy. *The Gospel of Luke* (Collegeville, MN: The Liturgical Press, 2006).

Tarazi, Paul N. *The New Testament Introduction: Luke and Acts.* Crestwood, NY: St. Vladimir's Seminary Press, 2001.

ABOUT THE AUTHOR

Fr. William Mills, Ph.D. is the rector of the Nativity of the Holy Virgin Orthodox Church in Charlotte, NC. Fr. Mills received his Bachelor of History from Millersville University of Pennsylvania and then pursued theological studies at Saint Vladimir's Orthodox Theological Seminary in Crestwood, NY where he received both a Master of Divinity and Master of Theology degrees. He then pursued advanced theological studies at the Union Institute and University in Cincinnati, Ohio where he received his doctorate in Pastoral Theology. Fr. Mills is available for parish and clergy retreats. He is also a founding member of the Orthodox Center for the Advancement of Biblical Studies (www.ocabs.org). You can visit his personal website at www.williamcmills.com.

www.ingramcontent.com/pod-product-compliance
Lightning Source LLC
LaVergne TN
LVHW011400080426
835511LV00005B/368